Accounting for Casinos and Gaming

Steven M. Bragg

For more information about AccountingTools® products, visit our Web site at www.accountingtools.com.

ISBN-13: 978-1-938910-67-8

Printed in the United States of America

Table of Contents

iv

Preface

The gaming industry is a unique environment for the accountant. There is far more cash than is normally found in most organizations, plus a number of different transactions to account for – jackpots, loyalty programs, gaming chips, comps, and more. The result can be bewildering for the accountant. The *Accounting for Casinos and Gaming* book is designed to bring clarity to the situation by providing an overview of gaming operations, and describing those accounting issues most relevant to a gaming entity.

The book is divided into three sections. In Chapter 1, we describe the elements of a gaming business and how it is organized. In Chapters 2 through 8, we start with the system of accounting and then progress through all of the accounting topics that may apply to a casino, including the derivation of gaming revenue, transfer pricing, payroll, and fixed asset accounting. In Chapters 9 through 11, we describe the many controls and policies needed to reduce the risk of loss, as well as those gaming-specific aspects of financial reports and disclosures, and federally-mandated currency reporting.

You can find the answers to many questions about the accounting for casinos and gaming in the following chapters, including:

- How is a casino organized?
- What is the most appropriate accounting for promotions?
- What is the accounting for a gaming license?
- What are the steps required to prepare a payroll?
- What are the special considerations when collecting overdue debt from customers?
- How is the cost of interest capitalized into a newly-constructed casino?
- What types of controls are needed on the casino floor?
- What are the obligations of a casino when reporting currency transactions to the government?

The *Accounting for Casinos and Gaming* book is designed for students and professionals, who can use it to gain an understanding of accounting operations in the gaming industry.

Centennial, Colorado
January 2016

About the Author

Steven Bragg, CPA, has been the chief financial officer or controller of four companies, as well as a consulting manager at Ernst & Young. He received a master's degree in finance from Bentley College, an MBA from Babson College, and a Bachelor's degree in Economics from the University of Maine. He has been a two-time president of the Colorado Mountain Club, and is an avid alpine skier, mountain biker, and certified master diver. Mr. Bragg resides in Centennial, Colorado. He has written the following books and courses:

Accountants' Guidebook
Accounting Changes and Error Corrections
Accounting Controls Guidebook
Accounting for Casinos and Gaming
Accounting for Derivatives and Hedges
Accounting for Earnings per Share
Accounting for Inventory
Accounting for Investments
Accounting for Managers
Accounting for Stock-Based Compensation
Accounting Procedures Guidebook
Bookkeeping Guidebook
Budgeting
Business Combinations and Consolidations
Business Insurance Fundamentals
Business Ratios
Business Valuation
Capital Budgeting
CFO Guidebook
Closing the Books
Constraint Management
Corporate Cash Management
Corporate Finance
Cost Accounting Fundamentals
Cost Management Guidebook
Credit & Collection Guidebook
Developing and Managing Teams
Enterprise Risk Management
Fair Value Accounting

Financial Analysis
Financial Forecasting and Modeling
Fixed Asset Accounting
Foreign Currency Accounting
GAAP Guidebook
Hospitality Accounting
Human Resources Guidebook
IFRS Guidebook
Interpretation of Financial Statements
Inventory Management
Investor Relations Guidebook
Lean Accounting Guidebook
Mergers & Acquisitions
New Controller Guidebook
Nonprofit Accounting
Payables Management
Payroll Management
Project Accounting
Public Company Accounting
Purchasing Guidebook
Real Estate Accounting
Recruiting and Hiring
Revenue Recognition
The Soft Close
The Statement of Cash Flows
The Year-End Close
Treasurer's Guidebook
Working Capital Management

On-Line Resources by Steven Bragg

Steven maintains the accountingtools.com web site, which contains continuing professional education courses, the Accounting Best Practices podcast, and hundreds of articles on accounting subjects.

Accounting for Casinos and Gaming is also available as a continuing professional education (CPE) course. You can purchase the course (and many other courses) and take an on-line exam at:

www.accountingtools.com/cpe

Chapter 1
Gaming Operations

Introduction

Legalized gambling is allowed in some form in many parts of the world. Gambling can be conducted in a multitude of venues, including fixed facilities, on riverboats, and on cruise ships. Gambling may also be integrated into other activities as an ancillary function. For example, race tracks have added gambling operations to such an extent that their designation has been altered to *racinos*. Examples of gambling activities include:

- Casino gambling
- Dog race betting
- Horse race betting
- Jai alai
- Native American gaming
- Riverboat gaming
- State lotteries

Many of these gambling activities are integrated into large-scale hotel, restaurant, and convention operations that are designed to attract visitors for extended periods of time. The gaming commissions that oversee casinos may require a full-service approach, mandating a certain minimum number of hotel rooms, to ensure that casinos generate a sufficient volume of customer traffic to remain in business.

Riverboats may be required to engage in a certain amount of cruising. However, this entails a substantial additional cost, since a riverboat must be seaworthy, and have a captain and crew. In general, riverboat owners prefer to keep their boats docked as much as possible in order to cut down on the extra expense. A variation is the barge, which has a casino built onto it, and which is not expected to cruise. Instead, a barge is permanently moored. The other services offered by such casinos are then maintained on shore, such as hotel and food service operations. The adaptation of boats and barges into casino operations can be tricky, since they must pass seaworthiness ratings.

The number of gaming entities allowed to do business in a state is a function of the laissez faire attitude of the state government. If the state is willing to open its doors to gaming, then there is a proliferation of gaming entities. Conversely, if the government considers gaming to be an activity that should be tightly controlled, then it will only grant a limited number of gaming licenses, effectively creating an oligopoly for the few lucky license recipients. In the former case, the gaming tax (which is applied as a percentage of revenue) tends to be quite low, whereas the tax may be three times higher in a state where only a few licenses have been granted. In effect, gaming companies granted licenses in a restrictive state must understand that competition will be restricted, but that the restriction comes at a price.

Types of Games

There are many types of games that a gaming establishment might offer to its customers. Here are the most common, along with brief descriptions:

- *Table games*. As the name indicates, these games are played at a table, where players wager against the house, and a dealer manages the game. Examples of table games are baccarat, blackjack, craps, and roulette.
- *Card games*. These are games in which customers wager against each other, rather than against the house.
- *Slot machines*. These devices require a monetary input to activate, and then generate a winning combination of symbols at random, which triggers the payment of a jackpot. The concept has expanded over time to include all types of electronic gaming devices. Examples of slot machines are reel spinners, video slot machines, video poker, and progressive slots.
- *Keno*. This game uses a ball machine or a random number generator to derive a set of numbers between 1 and 80. Customers guess which numbers will be selected.
- *Bingo*. This is a game in which customers buy bingo cards that contain a 5×5 grid of numbers. As random numbers are called out, they mark whichever numbers are present on their cards. The first person to complete a row or column on a card is the winner.
- *Race and sports betting*. This is a betting operation in which customers bet on the outcome of a race or sports event.

There are two general types of games. A *banked game* is one in which the gaming organization participates in games of chance with its customers, where both parties have the opportunity to win or lose money based on the outcome of the games. There are also *gaming related activities*, where the gaming organization receives a fee for administering the game, rather than being at risk of winning or losing based on the outcome of the games. Most activities conducted within a casino are of the banked game variety, such as table games, slot machines, and keno.

Casino Organizational Structure

The organizational structure of a gaming entity is key to its ability to maintain a high level of control over operations, assets, and cash flows. This tends to result in a hierarchical organizational structure, where there are a number of managers to oversee operations. We explore different levels of the organizational structure of a casino in the following sub-section, followed by a discussion of job titles and the physical organization of the entity.

Organization Charts

In the following high-level organization chart for a casino, we emphasize the listing of direct reports to the chief financial officer (CFO).

Sample Casino Organizational Structure

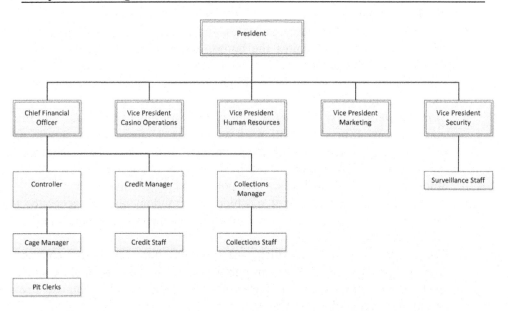

In particular, note that the vice president of security does not have a reporting relationship with any of the other senior management positions, instead reporting straight to the president. This arrangement is used so that the surveillance staff can look for violations not only by customers, but also by other members of the casino staff.

The CFO occupies a prominent place in this organizational structure, because of the large amounts of cash moving through the business and the large number of controls needed throughout the operations. Of particular importance is the extension of credit to customers and the collection of the resulting receivables.

The preceding organization chart emphasized only those accounting functions unique to a casino. In the following chart, we expand the view of the accounting function to include all other accounting activities. Also note how the purchasing, human resources, and information technology functions can be clustered under the controller; this is because a casino may not provide a separate reporting structure for these functions.

Sample Accounting Organizational Structure – Departmental View

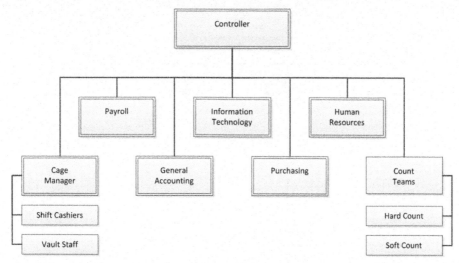

Another way of looking at the organizational structure of the accounting department is where they are located within the casino. Some positions are involved with casino operations to record transactions and move money and chips to and from the casino floor. Other employees work within the cage, such as cashiers and credit staff, while count teams (as the name implies) are involved with counting the drops being received from the casino floor. All remaining accounting employees work in the general accounting area. From this perspective, the organization structure looks like the following illustration.

Sample Organizational Structure – Locational View

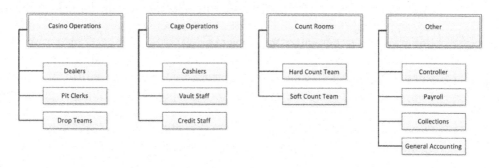

In the next organization chart, we drill down into the responsibilities of the vice president of casino operations. This chart is needed in order to understand the controls that must be applied to the various functions of the business. Controls are discussed in the Controls and Policies chapter.

Sample Casino Operations Organizational Structure

```
                          ┌──────────────────┐
                          │  Vice President   │
                          │ Casino Operations │
                          └──────────────────┘
```

Slot Manager	Games Manager	Poker Manager	Director of Race & Sports

Slot Mechanic

Control Room

Shift Manager	Shift Manager	Shift Manager	Shift Manager

| Floor Person | Pit Manager | Cashier | Dealers | Cashier | Mutuel Clerks |

| Change Clerk | Coin Booth Cashier | Floor Person |

Dealer

Job Titles

Brief descriptions of the more specialized job titles noted in the preceding organization charts are as follows:

Shift Managers

- *Shift manager (slots).* Responsible for the operation of all slot machines and the supporting personnel for a shift. Also responsible for the positioning of slot machines to maximize their revenue.
- *Shift manager (games).* Responsible for the operation of all gaming tables, and the employees staffing and supporting the tables for a shift.
- *Shift manager (poker).* Responsible for the operation of all poker games for a shift.
- *Shift manager (race and sports).* Responsible for race and sports book operations, as well as updates to event information for a shift.

Other Positions

- *Cashier (race and sports).* Pays customers for winning tickets.
- *Change clerk (slots).* Makes change for customers in the slot machine area and assists with jackpot payoffs.
- *Coin booth cashier (slots).* Pays out jackpots from slot machines and makes change.

- *Dealer (games and poker).* Responsible for the games at a specific table. Also monitors rules compliance.
- *Floor person (games).* Supervises the dealers at a group of tables. Also monitors rules compliance.
- *Floor person (slots).* Supervises the coin booth cashiers and change clerks. Also verifies jackpot payouts.
- *Mutuel clerk (race and sports).* Accepts wagers from customers.
- *Pit clerk (games).* Completes all transactions in a pit, such as credits, fills, and markers.
- *Pit manager (games).* Oversees all table game operations in a specific pit.
- *Slot mechanic (slots).* Maintains all slot machines and updates related paperwork.

Physical Organization - Casino

We have thus far described a number of positions within a casino, but have not addressed the physical organization of the entity. At a high level, a casino is divided into the casino floor and the casino cage.

The casino floor is where all gaming activity occurs. It may be sub-divided into several areas, such as gaming pits and slot zones. A gaming pit is a section of the casino floor that is encircled by gaming tables, and which is administered by a group of casino personnel. Each gaming pit may specialize in a particular type of game, or there may be tables offering several different games. A slot zone is a section of the gaming floor that is dedicated to slot machines. Each slot zone typically includes a coin booth, where customers can buy or redeem tokens, slot markers are issued or redeemed, and jackpots can be collected. A casino may also contain a number of side rooms that deal with other gaming activities, such as race and sports betting, bingo, poker, and keno.

The casino cage is essentially the in-house bank of a casino. It contains the cashiers and the casino's inventory of chips and currency. The cashiers provide banking services and record all financial transactions. Examples of the services provided by the cage to customers are:

- Open deposit and credit accounts
- Deposit and withdraw funds
- Receive and pay off markers
- Purchase and cash checks
- Issue and receive funds by wire transfer
- Redeem chips
- Exchange currency

A common activity for the cage staff is to accept *front money*, which is a cash deposit by a customer that will be used for gaming purposes. A player can then sign markers at table games that will draw down the amount of front money.

Customers can deposit funds directly into a wagering account. They can then transfer these funds electronically from the account to any slot machine on the premises. Once they have concluded their gaming activities, they can transfer any remaining funds (or increased funds, if there has been a jackpot) back to their wagering account.

If a customer only wants to have the cash held at the cage for convenience purposes, then it is known as *safekeeping money*.

In a larger casino, there may be several smaller cages that are strategically placed to service particular areas of the casino floor, such as slot zones, betting parlors, and high roller areas. Eventually, all funds related to the casino floor flow through a cage.

The functions of a cage are usually subdivided into several components, which are:

- *Main bank*. All currency is stored in this location. Currency flows from the gaming tables and cashiers' windows to the main bank, and from there to the casino's commercial bank. The main bank also maintains an inventory of coins to support operations on the casino floor.
- *Cashier windows*. These are the locations through which cashiers interact with customers. There may be a number of windows, depending on the volume of customer interaction during peak periods.
- *Chip bank*. Gaming chips are stored in this location, which is also known as the fill bank. All chips flow from this location to and from the gaming tables and cashiers' windows. For example, chips are sent to a cashier's window to refill depleted chip inventories. The chip bank also accepts returns of excess chips from a cashier's window that result from chip redemptions. All chip transactions are documented, so that the amount on hand can be reconciled at any time.
- *Credit management*. All credit accounts are managed in this location, including decisions to extend credit.
- *Marker bank*. All marker activity (customer debts and repayments) is recorded in this area. The staff monitors the inventory of issued markers that have been forwarded from the table games, as well as front money, safekeeping deposits, and similar items.

All bills, coins, chips, and tokens not currently in use within the casino are stored in the vault. The vault staff engages in the following functions:

- *Inflow from count rooms*. Bills and coins are shifted from the count rooms to the vault. The vault staff verifies the count sheets associated with each transfer of bills and coins, and then stores them within the vault.
- *Outflow to bank and back to casino*. The vault personnel periodically determines the amount of excess bills on hand, and arranges to have this amount transported to the bank. Coins are not typically transported out of the casino, given their weight. Instead, coins are recirculated through the casino, in order to make change for customers using the slot machines.
- *Foreign chips*. Any chips issued by other casinos and accepted on the casino floor are stored in the vault. These chips are eventually presented to the originating casinos for reimbursement.

- *Foreign currency*. Foreign currency exchanged by customers is held in the vault until it can be converted back into dollars.
- *Chips and tokens*. Reserve chips are kept in the vault, as well as special chips that are used in tournaments.
- *Accounting interface*. The vault staff informs the accounting staff of the bill and coin totals it has received, which is used to derive the revenue figure for the casino.

The total amount of currency kept in the vault is fairly consistent over time. Any excess currency from winnings is offloaded to the casino's bank. A minimum level must be kept on hand to cover any shortfalls caused by customer winnings.

Physical Organization – Card Room

In card rooms, players gamble against each other. There are no house-banked games. In a card room, there are usually two general categories of games, which are:
- Poker games
- California games, where one player acts as the bank and the other players bet against the bank. The banker collects the winning bets and pays all losing bets.

In a card room, the physical organization is similar to the layout of a casino gaming pit. Dealers still conduct the games, and are supervised by floor persons. However, there are a number of differences from the casino format, such as:
- A card club does not provide complimentary items (comps) to attract its best customers
- Chip runners are used who sell chips directly to and redeem the chips from customers
- Card clubs earn money from table fees, not from player wins or losses. The fee could be a fixed commission rate (known as a *rake-off*) or a playing time rental rate. Consequently, and also because of the lack of comps, there is no player rating system (as described in the next section).
- Dealers buy the inventory of their chip tray from the card room. Since they own this inventory, they may be allowed to gamble during breaks, and sometimes while dealing a game.

The rake-off from each hand is deposited in a table drop box (see the Table Drop Boxes section). Normal gaming table drop and count procedures are then applied to the drop box.

A card room has a cage that offers services similar to those offered by a casino cage.

Table Game Operations

In the following sub-sections, we cover the basic flow of transactions in a table game, including fills, credits, and reconcilations.

Table Inventory

A rack of chips is maintained at each table game, so that players can be paid on winning wagers. The amount and denomination of these chips is referred to as the *table inventory*. A different chip denomination is stored in each row of the rack. The dealer may place a clear plastic disc at regular intervals in each row, which makes it easier to count the number of chips in the row. For example, a disc may be inserted after every 20 $5 chips, to delineate a block of $100 of chips.

At the start of the day, a rack will contain a certain number of chips of each denomination. Over time, the dealer pays out winning bets from this rack and replenishes it with losing bets. Because the house has a small percentage advantage on all games played, the number of chips in the rack should increase over time. However, customers may pay for chips with cash or markers at the table, which depletes the table inventory. If chips are bought with cash, the dealer issues an equivalent number of chips and then drops the cash into the table's drop box. If the customer wants to redeem chips, he takes the chips to the cage to cash out. A customer does not redeem chips from a dealer.

Fill Transactions

A large payout may require the rack to be replenished. If so, chips are sent to the table from the cage, which is known as a *fill*. A fill transaction is initiated by a request for fill form, which may be an electronic transaction that is initiated by a pit supervisor and sent to the cage. This form is not prepared by the dealer, to maintain a separation of duties. The cage staff assembles the requested number of chips and then notifies the security department that it needs a pickup for a fill. At this time, the cage cashier also prepares a multi-part fill slip, which is a prenumbered document. A security officer is sent to the fill window of the cage, where he counts and verifies the chips that are to be delivered to the requesting table. Both the cashier and the security officer sign the fill slip. The original fill slip goes with the chips, with the other copies being retained in the cage. The security officer then takes the chips to the table needing replenishment. The pit supervisor matches the amount of the fill slip to the amount originally requested on the request for fill form, and staples the two forms together. In the presence of the pit supervisors and security officer, the dealer counts the received chips and signs the fill slip to verify receipt. The combined fill slip and request for fill form goes into the drop box. There may be an additional copy of the fill slip that is returned to the cage by the security officer.

A fill is essentially a payout, since the only reason for a fill is that players are winning more than they are losing. Consequently, a fill slip is treated as a documented pay out when the contents of a drop box are counted.

Credit Slip Transactions

If there are excess chips in the rack, a multi-part *credit slip* is prepared by a pit supervisor and sent to the cage, which authorizes the security staff to collect the overage and move them to the cage. A security officer collects the required number of chip racks from the cage and a copy of the credit slip, and takes them to the indicated table. In the presence of the pit supervisor, the dealer takes the racks and slip from the security officer, counts the chips to be removed, and places them in the racks. The security officer counts the racks to verify that the amounts are correct. Then the dealer and security officer sign the credit slip. The dealer then drops the completed form into the drop box, while the security officer takes the chips to the cage. At the cage, the cage cashier verifies the chip count in the racks and then signs the original credit slip to accept the chips. A credit is considered a payout reduction.

When chips are transported between the cage and table game, every party involved (including the transporting security guard) signs off on the associated slip. Doing so means that each person in turn accepts responsibility for the chips.

It is possible that chips could be shifted from one table game to another, which is called a *cross-fill*. This could make sense when there is a chip shortage on one table and a surplus on another. However, due to the increased level of difficulty in reconciling chip counts by table, cross-fills are discouraged.

Ending Reconciliation

Whenever there is a shift change or a table closes, the responsible dealer and floor person jointly reconcile the table inventory to what was reported at the end of the last shift, using a table inventory card to tabulate the ending table inventory. The ending chip balances are entered into a master game report. When there is a change in the beginning and ending table inventory, this constitutes a change in the table's gross gaming revenue.

The calculation of gross gaming revenue for a table includes the following factors:

+	Cash
+	Markers issued
+	Credit received for chips returned to the cage
+	Ending table inventory
-	Fills received from the cage
-	Beginning table inventory
=	Table gross gaming revenue

The table inventory card is a two-part form. Once complete, the first part of the form is placed in the drop box before the box is removed from the table at the end of a shift or gaming day. The second part of the form is placed in the replacement drop box that accumulates documents and currency for the next shift or gaming day. This approach allows for the preceding calculation of gross gaming revenue to be made, since the beginning and ending table inventory information is then available for each shift.

The use of a table inventory card keeps a revenue calculation from inadvertently including a simple exchange of bills for chips, rather than an actual win transaction for the casino. For example, $20 may appear in the drop box, which one might reasonably assume constitutes a win for the casino. However, the actual transaction might have been a customer exchanging a $20 bill for a chip of the same denomination without engaging in any play, which merely results in a change in the table inventory, rather than a win for the casino.

EXAMPLE

A gaming table experiences a number of transactions during a shift, as outlined in the following table. The table notes the derivation of gross gaming revenue.

Cash in drop box		$7,400
Markers issued		5,000
Total drop		12,400
Chip transfers		
Fills	-$2,500	
Credits	1,500	
Net chip transfers		-1,000
Table inventory change		
Beginning table inventory	-15,000	
Ending table inventory	14,200	
Table inventory net change		-800
Gross gaming revenue (win)		$10,600

The information in the table appears on the master gaming report for the gaming table.

Foreign Chips

An additional complication to table game operations is the presence of *foreign chips*. These are chips that have been issued by other casinos. A customer may bring in foreign chips and be allowed to play them at a table game. If a customer plays these chips and loses them, the dealer puts them in the drop box. During the subsequent counting process, these chips are set aside and later presented to the issuing casino for reimbursement in cash. Foreign chips are not always allowed in casinos, either by management policy or the dictates of the applicable gaming commission.

Player Rating System

A player rating system (PRS) tracks the gaming activity of a casino's customers. A floor person prepares a player rating card for each rated customer at a table, which is later added to the PRS database. The rating card identifies a customer, pit and table location, and the amount of currency received from the customer in the form of cash bets and for the purchase of chips. The estimated average bet and hours played are also noted.

The intent of a PRS is to make a determination from gaming activity regarding the level of complimentary services that will be offered to certain customers in order to entice them to play further. Customers who spend a large amount of time (and money) are given a high club status, such as being in a gold club, executive club, and so forth. Each of these club levels comes with a different set of complimentary benefits, or *comps*, such as faster check-in, upgrades to hotel suites, free meals, and so forth.

Table Drop Boxes

A casino does not record the results of an individual gaming transaction with its customers. Doing so would require an inordinate amount of clerical time, and would also delay the games, which in turn would reduce revenue. Instead, it must wait until the end of the shift or gaming day to examine the contents of the drop box that is linked to each gaming table. Each drop box is securely locked under a gaming table; the dealer drops into it all cash and paperwork generated by a game. The drop box contains a number of items, including:

- Currency
- Coupons
- Fill and credit slips
- Markers
- Requests for fills and credits

There should not be any chips or tokens in a lock box.

The drop box is essential to the reporting of revenue by a casino, since it contains the aggregate activity of a gaming table. The following process flow enumerates how a drop box is handled:

1. An empty drop box is removed from the count room at the beginning of the shift or gaming day and is taken to a gaming table by a *drop team*. Each drop box is marked with a unique identifying number for the table with which it is associated. When each new drop box arrives at a table, the old drop box is removed and taken back to the count room. A key is needed to remove the box. There are multiple drop boxes on the casino floor, so a trolley is used to transport the empty boxes in bulk to the casino floor, and to bring back filled drop boxes.
2. A count team assembles in the count room, and verifies that all drop boxes have been accounted for.

3. A team of counters opens each box with a key (different from the one used to remove the box from the table) and counts the contents, typically with two people independently counting the contents. Counting machines are used to automatically count bills and coins.

4. The count team signs off on the final count report to significant that they are in agreement with the total.

5. The drop box contents are then shifted to the vault. However, the vault staff will not accept the funds until it verifies the contents, so a vault representative conducts an independent count, not knowing the results of the first count. If all is in order, the vault representative signs a transfer form for the funds, and security moves the funds to the vault.

6. The signed count report and transfer form are then transferred to the accounting department.

Slot Machine Operations

When a casino offers coin-operated slot machines, its first concern is to ensure that customers have a sufficient number of coins with which to play the machines. There are several ways to do so. Customers can go to a cage cashier and swap their bills for coins. However, this involves movement by customers, and experience has shown that customers will spend more if they have to travel less to swap their bills for coins. Consequently, there may be a coin booth located adjacent to or in the midst of the slot machines, where an inventory of coins or tokens is kept for ready exchange with customers. The most customer-centric approach of all is to have change personnel roaming the slots area, providing change as needed, and returning periodically to the coin booth to swap out their excess bills for more coins. This latter approach tends to generate the highest revenue, since it encourages customers to continue playing without interruption. We now move to what happens when coins are inserted into a slot machine.

A traditional slot machine accepts coins which first fall into a hopper. The hopper is intended to hold a certain amount of coins that are then used to pay jackpots. Once the hopper is filled by coin insertions from customers, all additional coins are redirected into a storage box at the bottom of the machine, which is periodically emptied. The hopper is positioned above the payout tray, so that gravity can be used to drop payout coins into the tray. The storage box is located below the payout tray, and so cannot be used as a source of coins for jackpots.

When a customer wins a jackpot, the machine accesses the hopper and issues the required number of coins to the customer. If the hopper is emptied before the full amount of the jackpot has been paid (called a *short pay*), the machine alerts the change person with a bell and flashing light. The change person on duty verifies that the hopper is indeed empty, checks a meter inside the machine to determine how much of the jackpot has already been paid, and then takes these steps:

1. The change person goes to the cage and completes a jackpot payout slip that documents the remaining amount to pay the customer. The employee also completes a fill form for the coins needed to refill the slot machine's hopper.

2. The cage staff assembles the requested funds, counts them, enters the amount on the two forms, and signs them. The change person verifies the count and then signs the form to accept responsibility for the funds.
3. The change person pays the customer the remaining amount of the jackpot. With security monitoring, the employee then opens the slot and puts the remainder of the coins in the hopper. The change person then puts his copies of the fill slip and the jackpot payout slip in the storage box at the bottom of the slot machine.

Many slot machines include the Ticket In Ticket Out (TITO) system. When a customer wants to cash out of a slot machine, he presses the Cash Out button and the machine prints a TITO ticket, which contains a bar coded dollar amount. This ticket can then be used to drop money into a different slot machine, or it can be taken to the cage to cash out. The advantage of this system to the casino is that far fewer coins need to be collected and counted as part of a hard drop (see the Slot Drop section), while fewer change persons are needed to make change or pay out jackpots.

> **Note:** The change personnel can be equipped with portable terminals to verify tickets, and cash out smaller amounts. This is more convenient for customers, and reduces the work load of the cage cashiers.

If TITO is prevalent throughout a casino, the amount of currency handled may drop so precipitously that the hard count and soft count teams can be combined, which reduces payroll costs while still maintaining an adequate level of control over slot drops.

Additional issues related to slot machine operations are as follows:

- *Initial hopper load.* The hopper on a newly-installed slot machine must be filled with a minimum amount of coins, so that the coins are available for a payout if a customer wins a jackpot before ongoing operations naturally fill the hopper. This initial transfer of coins from the cage to the slot machines is not recorded as a revenue deduction. Instead, it is noted in the accounting records as a transfer of cash from the cage to the slot hoppers, which is a transfer from an asset account to another asset account.

- *Hopper load creep.* It is possible for the amount of coins stored in a hopper to gradually increase above the initial load amount over time, perhaps due to an initially low count or because of machine error in overfilling the hopper. Whatever the reason, this issue can be detected by periodically conducting hopper counts. When there is a case of hopper overfill, the excess is removed and counted as additional revenue.

- *Subsequent hopper fills.* A hopper may be completely emptied by the pay out of a jackpot. If so, a request is made to the cage to provide sufficient coins to re-fill the hopper. The accounting for a hopper fill is the same as was used for the initial hopper load.

- *Coin-in*. The traditional measure of slot machine performance is *coin-in*, which is the amount of coins put into a slot machine by customers. The definition can be expanded in those cases where TITO and bill acceptors are used, in which case coin-in is considered to be the total amount played on a slot machine by a customer.
- *Paid out*. The offset to coin-in is the amount *paid out*, which is the amount paid to customers for jackpots won. This payment can take a variety of forms, such as coins directly paid from the slot machine, an additional payment made from the coin booth, or a voucher that can be cashed in or used for additional play.

Tokens

Tokens are used instead of coins in order to avoid the need to swap out the coin receptacle when coins of a new size are issued. The last time this was a problem was when the Susan B. Anthony $1 coin was issued, which was smaller than the Eisenhower coin that it replaced. Instead, the coin receptacle is configured for a standard-sized $1 token that is under the control of the casino, and which is therefore not expected to change.

Customers swap their money for tokens, which the casino only recognizes as revenue after they have been recovered from slot machines as part of the slot drop process. Some tokens are never recovered, either because they are lost by customers or retained as souvenirs. In the event of non-recovery, tokens are subject to breakage accounting, where a portion of the lost tokens are eventually recognized as revenue. See the Gaming-Specific Accounting chapter for more information.

Slot Clubs

A casino usually has a slot club, which is a tracking system that it uses to monitor the activity of its higher-volume slot machine players. The resulting information can be used to encourage these players to continue playing, usually by offering points that are linked to the amount paid into the slot machines. As a customer cumulatively pays more into slot machines, the person is shifted into a higher reward level. The points can be used for cash-back awards or shopping points that can be used to buy merchandise offered by the casino. A variation on the concept is to award random bonuses to slot club members, which provides an incentive for infrequent slot users to still enroll in a slot club program on the off chance that they could still win a jackpot. The award of a random bonus on the casino floor also elevates the level of excitement, encouraging more people to play.

Slot Drop

The amount of currency retained by a slot machine, not including the amount retained in the hopper for payouts, is called the *slot drop*. This money is transferred to the vault through a pair of processes called the hard drop and soft drop, where the hard drop transfers and counts coins, while the soft drop transfers and counts bills.

If the coin volume in a slot machine has historically been low, the slot drop may happen at fairly long intervals, typically on a day when customer activity is lowest, so that customers are not inconvenienced by the interruption. Since more customers tend to use bills than coins, the currency acceptor may be dropped daily, even though the coin drop is scheduled at longer intervals. The time of day for a slot drop is usually quite early, when customer activity is lowest.

The counting process for currency removed from slot machines is different from what is used for table drop boxes, because the slot machines have automated internal counters that track the bills and coins inserted into them. The hard drop and soft drop process flows are noted in the following sub-sections.

Hard Drop

The coins and tokens that have been put into a slot machine by customers are called the hard drop. The hard drop is stored in two receptacles in a slot machine. The default storage receptacle is the hopper, which is employed by the slot machine to issue jackpots below a predetermined threshold level. Once the number of coins and tokens exceeds the amount allowed in the hopper, any excess is routed to a drop bucket within the machine. Only the amount in the drop bucket needs to be removed, since (as just noted) the amount in the hopper is expected to be used for payouts. The following process flow enumerates how the drop bucket is handled:

1. The hard drop team signs out the key to the hard count storage room, noting the sign-out time. The team removes from this room the drop buckets needed to replace the buckets it plans to swap out of the slot machines.
2. The team then signs out the keys to the targeted slot machines, noting the sign-out time.
3. The team opens each slot machine in turn, removes its bucket, and replaces it with an empty bucket, while being monitored and guarded by a security team. Each drop bucket is identified with a specific slot machine, so that the contents of the bucket can be traced back to a machine.
4. A member of the count team accesses the meters in the slot machine and writes down the current amounts on the meters, which note the coin-in and coin-out amounts. This information can be compared to the subsequent actual count.
5. The team returns the keys to the main cashier, who logs in the keys as having been received, as well as the time of day.
6. The bucket is taken to the hard count room, where it is weighed and the coins and tokens are automatically counted and wrapped. The wrapped amounts are then counted and summarized by denomination, and compared to the weigh totals to see if there are any variances to investigate. If the count team agrees that the resulting summarized count sheet is correct, they all sign the sheet, attesting to its accuracy.
7. The wrapped coins are then moved to storage cans and shifted to the vault, along with the associated summarization paperwork. However, the vault

staff will not accept the funds until it verifies the contents, so a vault representative conducts an independent count of the wrapped coins and tokens. If all is in order, the vault representative signs a transfer form for the funds, and security moves the funds to the vault, where it is stored in a coin vault area.

Currency Acceptor Drop

A currency acceptor (also called a bill validator) takes bills from customers at a slot machine, rather than coins and tokens, and converts the amount paid into credits on the machine. The process for shifting bills from currency acceptors to a counting room is similar to the hard drop process. The containers end up in a soft count room, and use the same counting procedure already described for table drop boxes. In this case, a high-speed bill counter is used to count and stack the bills. The key difference is that the slot machine's currency acceptor maintained a count of the bills received, which can now be compared to the actual count to see if there are any variances.

Slot Gaming Revenue Calculation

The gross gaming revenue associated with a slot machine is calculated in the following manner:

Drop compilation:		
Coins removed from drop bucket	$1,900	
Electronic funds transferred from wagering account to machine	1,000	
Total drop		$2,900
Issuances compilation:		
Fills	-500	
Electronic funds transferred to wagering account from machine	-800	
Hand paid jackpots	-600	
Tickets issued by machine	-400	
Change in hopper balance	-100	
Aggregate deductions		-2,400
Gross gaming revenue (win)		$500

The change in the hopper balance is noted in the preceding table for calculating gross gaming revenue. In reality, calculating this change is so labor-intensive that it is only tracked at relatively long intervals. In the interim, there is assumed to be no change in the hopper balance.

Keno Operations

Keno is a game of chance that is similar to lotto, and which uses a ball machine or a random number generator to derive a set of numbers between 1 and 80. Customers guess which numbers will be selected. The process flow for a keno bet and payout is:

1. A customer approaches the keno counter and states the numbers that he wants to bet on. The keno writer enters these numbers into the computer and issues a ticket that states the numbers entered into the system. The writer takes the customer's wager and places it in his cash drawer, along with a duplicate of the keno ticket.
2. After the keno drawing is complete and if the customer has won, the customer presents his winning ticket at the keno counter. The clerk verifies the ticket and pays out the winnings. The amount of the payout is entered into the computer.
3. At the end of the keno clerk's shift, he uses the keno ticket copies to balance his bank, along with the payout records in the computer. The net change in the clerk's bank represents the win or loss experienced by the casino.

A keno runner may be employed to take bets from customers elsewhere in the casino to the keno counter, and to bring any winnings back to the customers.

If the keno clerk runs low on money, as may occur when there is a big winner, a fill transaction can be used to obtain more money from the cage. In this case, a request for fill form is transmitted to the cage, where a cashier prepares a fill slip (as previously described for table game operations). The main difference between a table game fill and a keno fill is that currency is sent to the keno clerk, rather than chips.

Because all keno wagers and payouts are entered directly into the computer system, the casino always knows the exact status of all drops and payouts in the keno area.

Race and Sports Book Operations

The documentation flow for race and sports book operations is essentially the same as what was just described for keno. A customer places a bet at the betting window, and receives a ticket in exchange. The sportsbook agent keeps a second copy of the ticket. In the event of a win, the customer presents his ticket at the betting window, and is paid after the cashier verifies the win and matches the presented ticket with the original. The bet and payout records are needed by the cashier at the end of his shift to balance his bank.

If the cashier runs low on money, as may occur when there is a big winner, a fill transaction can be used to obtain more money from the cage. In this case, a request for fill form is transmitted to the cage, where a cashier prepares a fill slip (as previously described for table game operations). The main difference between a

18

table game fill and a race and sports book fill is that currency is sent to the cashier, rather than chips.

Bingo Operations

The documentation flow for bingo is somewhat different from what is used for keno or race and sports book operations, which is driven by the nature of the game. In bingo, the forms used by customers are associated with a specific bingo session, using a unique identification number. They buy bingo paper at the bingo cashier's window; the money collected by the casino is used to pay jackpots for anyone participating in that session. The casino makes money through the sale of bingo cards.

In a bingo game, one of 75 balls is drawn at random and announced. Participants check their cards to see if each called number is listed on their cards. Once someone has covered a specific pattern on their card (such as a row or column), they win the game.

When someone wins a bingo game, the bingo agent confirms that the numbers on a bingo form are indeed winning numbers. The bingo agent then verifies with the cashier that the identification number on the form is associated with the current bingo session. If so, the cashier pays out the jackpot. Documentation of the paper purchases and jackpot are needed by the cashier at the end of his shift to balance his bank.

At the end of bingo operations, the bingo clerks tally their cash in and paid out amounts. The net residual balance is the revenue generated by the casino.

Casino Credit

A casino may choose to grant credit to its best customers. Doing so increases revenues, since customers might otherwise not choose to gamble in the absence of credit. A further incentive associated with the provision of credit to a customer is that the credit must be used. If a customer elects not to gamble, then the credit will be withdrawn. Thus, the extension of credit comes with a strong incentive to use it. There are several forms of casino credit, which are:

- *Cashed checks.* A casino pays out cash to a customer in exchange for a check, thereby taking on the risk that the check might bounce, or that a check has been forged. This risk is mitigated by shifting the risk to a check approval service in exchange for a fee.
- *Held checks.* A casino may agree to hold a check and cash it on a specified later date, such as one month later. By holding a check, a casino is at risk of loss for the entire amount of the check for a relatively long period of time. In addition, a held check may be used to offset an existing credit balance, thereby allowing the customer to continue playing with a replenished credit. In this case, the casino's risk has increased to include both the amount of the held check and the amount of the additional credit used by the customer.

- *Credit line.* A credit line is the amount of credit that a casino is willing to extend to a customer for gaming purposes.

Prior to extending credit to a player, a casino should check the person's credit history. To do so, a customer is asked to fill out a credit application. The Nevada Gaming Control Board's Regulation 6 provides language that must be inserted into the credit application, making the customer's repayment responsibility clear:

> Each credit application must contain a statement approved by the chairman, separately signed by the patron, and in a font size of not less than 9 points, acknowledging the patron's understanding, that under Nevada law a credit instrument is the same as a personal check, and knowingly writing a credit instrument with insufficient funds in the account upon which it is drawn, or with intent to defraud, is a criminal act in the State of Nevada which may result in criminal prosecution. The following language, if used on a credit application, is deemed approved:

> "Warning: For the purposes of Nevada law, a credit instrument is identical to a personal check and may be deposited in or presented for payment to a bank or other financial institution on which the credit instrument is drawn. Willfully drawing or passing a credit instrument with the intent to defraud, including knowing that there are insufficient funds in an account upon which it may be drawn, is a crime in the State of Nevada which may result in criminal prosecution in addition to civil proceedings to collect the outstanding debt."

A credit application should contain at least the following information:
- Name and address
- Birth date
- Social security number
- Work information (where employed, job title, and business address)
- All applicable phone numbers
- Bank references and related account numbers
- Amount of credit requested
- Whether the person has declared bankruptcy in the past

While the preceding information can be taken down from a phone call or fax, a casino may insist on a person personally handing over a valid form of identification. A copy of this identification document can then be used to complete a currency transaction report (see the Financial Reports chapter).

Whether credit will be granted at all and the amount of the credit granted will vary, depending in part on the following issues:
- The information stated on a customer credit report, especially in regard to late unpaid balances, foreclosures, bankruptcies, tax liens, and civil judgments
- How long the customer has been playing at the casino
- The amount that the customer currently owes

- How long the reference bank account has been open
- The average balance in the reference bank account

If a customer already has established credit with other casinos, this credit history may be available through Central Credit LLC, which offers credit information services to member casinos. Central Credit can run credit checks on debts, marker activity, and repayment habits at all casinos where an applicant has a credit history.

The more detailed and gaming-specific information included in a Central Credit report can also reveal whether a customer has applied for credit at four or more casinos within the past two weeks. If this is the case, past credit history across the industry has shown that 80% of these "4 in 14" applicants will write checks that are rejected due to not sufficient funds. Thus, credit is usually denied to these applicants.

The key issues involved in extending casino credit are the ability of a customer to pay, as evidenced by the average bank balance or income records, and the customer's willingness to pay, as described in the Central Credit report. The average bank balance is a particularly valuable source of information, for it provides evidence of the liquid assets of a customer, which are those assets most likely to be used to pay off credit. For example, a casino may have found that it can reasonably expect to collect 100% of all markers if the credit granted does not exceed 15% of a customer's average bank balance. If so, this percentage could be applied as the basis for granting credit to all customers, perhaps with some variations to reflect the individual circumstances of certain customers.

The amount of credit granted will depend upon the willingness of a customer to play, where a strong record of play will warrant a larger credit. This propensity to play can be discerned from the past history of play with the casino, as well as from the amounts owed to other casinos as stated in the Central Credit report. There should be an in-house record for the more frequent players, which details the size of a player's bets, playing time, and winnings.

There are a number of additional considerations to assess when deciding upon the correct amount of credit to grant. These considerations are:

- *Long-term relations.* When evaluating the best amount of credit to grant a customer, the emphasis is on the word "best." Extending too much credit could lead a customer to default, in which case the person will likely be lost as a customer. The best credit level is one that the person can reasonably expect to repay, which means that he will be a returning customer.
- *Permanent or temporary credit.* Should the casino grant credit on a permanent basis, or only temporarily? It is safer to grant a temporary credit when a customer plays infrequently, since the individual's bank credit information may be outdated. Temporary credit may also be granted when prior payments were slow, but the casino management wants to give a customer an opportunity to pay at a faster rate in the future, thereby re-establishing his credit.
- *Credit during losses.* A customer may be suffering through a prolonged series of losses that has wiped out all existing credit, at which point the

player appeals for a temporary increase. These increases must be viewed with caution, for the losses may continue, resulting in a credit level that the customer cannot support. The extension of more credit is a particular concern when the customer has lost a large amount within a short period of time, or appears to be intoxicated. The amount actually extended should certainly be based on the customer's ability to repay, for which the best evidence is the average bank balance. If additional credit is granted, this incremental amount is almost always marked as "this trip only" in the customer's credit record, so that the credit level drops back to the original amount as soon as the person's current trip is over.

Tip: An interesting tactic when dealing with a request for credit increase is to first issue a customer a complimentary meal at the casino's restaurant, so that they have time to cool off and consider whether they really want to take on the risk of more debt.

It is possible that the input of the casino host department may be solicited as part of the credit granting decision. This group is interested in increasing gaming revenue, and so will present a case in favor of a higher credit level. Since the credit staff has a more conservative loss-protection orientation, it can be useful to obtain this more optimistic viewpoint, which can result in a more balanced consideration of the most appropriate credit level to grant.

Markers

A casino may offer credit to its customers. If so, the customers draw upon this credit by signing a marker. A marker is a check that is provided by the casino, and which may be structured to look similar to a bank check, with additional text regarding the customer's acceptance of the debt. The customer accepts the credit (and the underlying debt) when he signs the check. The Nevada Gaming Control Board requires in its Regulation 6 that the following text be inserted into a marker, which is intended to clarify a customer's repayment responsibilities:

> Each credit instrument must contain a notification, permanently and legibly printed on the face of the original credit instrument, in a font size of not less than 6 points, [which] notifies the patron of the requirements of Nevada law regarding personal checks. The following language, if used on a credit instrument, is deemed approved:

> "A credit instrument is identical to a personal check. Willfully drawing or passing a credit instrument knowing there are insufficient funds in an account upon which it may be drawn, or with the intent to defraud, is a crime in the State of Nevada which may result in criminal prosecution."

Markers are usually printed in the pit at the request of a customer. The pit supervisor asks the customer how much credit he wants; the supervisor then uses the casino's computer system to determine the amount of available credit for the person. If the requested amount is available, a marker is printed in the requested amount. Once the marker is printed, this reduces the remaining amount of available credit.

Once the customer signs a marker, he retains one copy, with the other copy going into the drop box at the table where the customer is playing. The customer is then given chips (not cash) equal to the amount of the marker.

A signed marker is a legally enforceable debt, so it is recorded by the accounting staff as an account receivable. A marker is not considered a loan, which would require the application of an interest charge to the outstanding balance. From a collection perspective (but not a profitability perspective), the best situation is for a customer to repay a marker from his winnings, so that the marker balance has been eliminated by the time the person has finished his gambling trip. If not, the casino must use its collections staff to obtain payment. Another possibility is that only part of a marker is repaid when a person leaves the casino. If so, the original marker is cancelled and replaced with one that contains the outstanding balance.

A customer may have brought funds with him to the casino and deposited it in the cage, which is called front money. This person will still be asked to sign a marker when he begins gaming activities, in order to be issued chips. The marker is immediately offset in the casino's computer system by the amount of the front money, so there is no debt outstanding.

Rim Play

A variation on markers is rim play. When rim play is allowed, customers are allowed to play without a marker until the end of play, at which point their losses are tallied and a marker is issued. The number of chips issued and the offsetting marker amounts are recorded on the player's rim card. Since a player could rack up substantial losses without having signed a marker, rim play represents a potentially uncollectible liability for a casino. Consequently, rim play is reserved only for high rollers, and is closely monitored by a supervisor.

Marketing Activities

A casino typically has quite an active marketing function, which is designed to bring customers to the casino, and to keep them playing there as long as possible. Here are several possible marketing activities that a casino may engage in:

Intended to Bring in Customers

- *Travel comps.* The casino offers to reimburse customers for their travel expenses to reach the casino.
- *Events.* The casino sponsors a slots or game tournament, and may also put up the prize money. The intent is to bring in players who will then continue to play at the casino.

Intended to Increase Playing Time

- *Free chips.* A casino may issue a number of non-negotiable chips to its customers for use at table games within the casino. These chips have no cash value, but their betting value is the same as the amount on regular chips. The dollar value of these chips is relatively low for the average customer, but could reach into the thousands of dollars for high rollers. Thus, the amount of promotional chips handed out can vary with the gaming activity or credit of customers. Promotional chips are given to customers for free. Customers are likely to wager all of these chips, since they cannot be redeemed for cash.
- *Match play coupons.* A casino may issue match play coupons to its customers. These coupons require a cash "match" from the customer before they can be used, which essentially doubles the amount of funding used by a customer, up to the maximum amount of the coupon. For example, a person could bet $20 and then use the coupon to double the amount of the bet to $40. These coupons typically expire within a short period of time, such as one month.

Cashier Reconciliations

When a cashier starts a shift, he is given a bank, which is a tray containing compartments for different denominations of currency and coins. A cage employee has already stocked the bank with a designated amount of bills and coins, and signs off on a form that states the amount in the bank. The cashier also counts the bank to verify the amounts, and signs off on the form, thereby taking over responsibility for the bank.

Cashiers typically operate under the imprest system, where their bank is set at a specific cash amount. Over the course of their shift, they will pay out cash for various reasons, such as a pay out to a customer for a jackpot. In return, they obtain a receipt from the payee, which takes the place of the cash in their bank. Similarly, they may exchange foreign currency, or make change for smaller denominations. By the end of their shift, the total of all their remaining cash and receipts should still be the same balance as at the beginning – it just has different components at the end of the shift, perhaps a large proportion of receipts, more bills, and fewer coins.

At the end of the shift, and perhaps at intervals during the shift, the cashier swaps the receipts with the main cashier for cash, thereby bringing the cash total back to the original amount. There may also be swaps of bills and coins with the main cashier to reconstitute the original mix of denominations for bills and coins.

The imprest balance may be increased in anticipation of high-volume periods, such as the weekend and holidays, and reduced back to a baseline level for all other periods.

At the end of the cashier's shift, the cashier counts the bank, including credit card receipts, and transfers the bank and count form to the cage employee. The cage employee conducts a separate count to verify the amounts, and also signs off on the form, thereby taking over responsibility for the bank.

Summary

In this chapter, we covered the organizational structure of a gaming operation, including table games, slot machines, keno, bingo, and race and sports book operations. We also addressed the credit issuance decision and the use of markers by customers, and finished with a discussion of the basic activities within the cage. In the following chapters, we move on to the system of accounting, as well as those accounting issues that are specific to gaming activities and other accounting topics that the controller of a casino is likely to face – such as the accounting for debt, fixed assets, interest capitalization, and payroll.

Chapter 2
The System of Accounting

Introduction

Before an accountant in the gaming industry can engage in accounting activities, it is first necessary to understand the basic underpinnings of accounting, as well as the general flow of accounting transactions. In this chapter, we describe the concept of an accounting framework and accounting principles, on which all accounting activities are based. We then give an overview of how accounting transactions are recorded and aggregated into financial statements, which involves the use of double entry accounting, journal entries, a chart of accounts, and ledgers. We conclude with a discussion of the accrual basis of accounting.

Financial Accounting Basics

This introductory section is intended to give an overview of financial accounting basics. Its orientation is toward recording financial information about a business.

First, what do we mean by "financial" accounting? This refers to the recordation of information about money. Thus, we will talk about issuing a marker to someone, as well as their payment of that marker, but we will not address any change in the value of a company's overall business, since the latter situation does not involve a specific transaction involving money.

A *transaction* is a business event that has a monetary impact, such as selling a hotel room or a meal to a customer or buying supplies from a vendor. In financial accounting, a transaction triggers the recording of information about the money involved in the event. For example, we would record in the accounting records such events (transactions) as:

- Incurring debt from a lender
- The receipt of an expense report from an employee
- Selling a meal to a customer
- Paying gaming taxes to the government
- Paying wages to employees

We record this information in *accounts*. An account is a separate, detailed record about a specific item, such as expenditures for office supplies, or accounts receivable, or accounts payable. There can be many accounts, of which the most common are:

Assets

- *Cash*. Includes bills and coins, bank checks, traveler's checks, money orders, cashier's checks, demand deposits, and similar instruments.
- *Marketable securities*. Includes all types of investments that are readily convertible into cash.
- *Receivables, casino*. Includes markers issued to customers that have not been repaid.
- *Receivables, notes*. Contains notes payable from customers that have had their markers converted into more formal notes, with scheduled payments and interest charges.
- *Receivables, trade*. Includes amounts due from other casino activities than gaming, such as hotel and restaurant billings.
- *Allowance for doubtful accounts*. Contains a reserve that is the best estimate of receivables that will not be collected. This is a contra account that is paired with and offsets the receivables accounts.
- *Prepaid expenses*. Includes payments made in advance for services that have not yet been consumed, such as insurance and advertising.
- *Food and beverage inventory*. Contains those inventory items used by the restaurant and bar segments of casino operations.
- *Fixed assets*. Contains the acquisition costs of all long-term assets, such as land, facilities, vehicles, computer systems, furniture and fixtures, and office equipment. There may be a separate account for each of these fixed asset classifications.
- *Accumulated depreciation*. Includes the aggregate amount of depreciation that has been charged against the fixed assets. This is a contra account that is paired with and offsets the fixed asset accounts.

Liabilities

- *Accounts payable*. Includes all obligations payable to suppliers.
- *Accrued expenses*. Contains expenses for which a supplier billing has not yet been received, but for which an obligation has been incurred.
- *Current portion of long-term debt*. Includes that portion of future debt payments that are due within the next 12 months.
- *Other current liabilities*. Includes all other obligations of the business that are payable in less than 12 months.
- *Long-term debt*. Includes all debt obligations of the entity that are due for payment in more than 12 months.
- *Other long-term liabilities*. Includes all obligations other debt that are payable in more than 12 months.

Equity

- *Capital stock.* Includes the amount at which shares were purchased from the company by investors. This line item may be split into common stock, preferred stock, and additional paid-in capital accounts, to provide more detail.
- *Retained earnings.* Includes the cumulative amount of all earnings to date, less shareholder dividends.
- *Treasury stock.* Contains the amount paid to investors to buy back their shares. This is a contra account that is paired with and offsets the receivables accounts.

Revenue

- *Gaming revenue.* Contains the total win from all pit games, slot machines, race betting and so forth.
- *Room revenue.* Includes revenue from any room rentals associated with the casino.
- *Complimentary rooms.* Includes the amount of any free rooms given away, recorded at their retail price.
- *Food sales.* Contains all paid meals and snacks served on the premises.
- *Complimentary food sales.* Includes the amount of any food given away, recorded at its retail price.
- *Beverage sales.* Includes all paid beverages served on the premises.
- *Complimentary beverage sales.* Includes the amount of any free drinks, recorded at their retail price.
- *Other sales.* Contains all ancillary sales, such as parking fees.

Expenses

- *Cost of food sales.* Includes the cost of food sold to customers, but not of the food service staff, which is included in the compensation expense account.
- *Cost of beverage sales.* Includes the cost of drinks sold to customers.
- *Compensation expense.* Includes the salaries and wages paid to employees, as well as any bonuses.
- *Benefits expense.* Includes the cost of providing benefits to employees, such as medical insurance, dental insurance, life insurance, and workers' compensation insurance.
- *Payroll taxes.* Includes the employer portion of all payroll taxes, including social security and Medicare taxes.
- *Bad debt expense.* Contains the estimated amount of losses from outstanding markers.
- *Uniforms.* Contains the costs to purchase, lease, and clean employee uniforms.
- *Utilities.* Includes the costs of electricity, gas, telephones, and Internet access.

- *Travel and entertainment.* Contains the travel and entertainment costs incurred by employees of the business.
- *Gaming supplies.* Includes the costs of all gaming consumables, such as dice, chips, and cards.
- *Repairs and maintenance.* Contains the expenses needed to keep gaming and related operations in the best possible condition.
- *Comps expense.* Each department is assigned at least one comps expense account, to which are charged the transfer prices on comps given to customers.
- *Licenses.* Includes the filing costs required to maintain all gaming, liquor, restaurant, and other licenses needed to stay in business.
- *Office supplies.* Contains the expenditures associated with lower-cost office supplies that are too inexpensive and consumed too rapidly to be considered fixed assets.
- *Miscellaneous.* Includes all expenses not large enough to be listed separately in their own account.

How do we enter information about transactions into these accounts? There are two ways to do so:
- *Software module entries.* If you use accounting software to record financial accounting transactions, there will probably be on-line forms to fill out for each of the major transactions, such as recording a supplier invoice. Every time you fill out one of these forms, the software automatically populates the accounts.
- *Journal entries.* You can access a journal entry form in the accounting software, or create a journal entry by hand. This is a more customized way to record accounting information.

The accounts are stored in the *general ledger*. This is the master set of all accounts, in which are stored all of the business transactions that have been entered into the accounts with journal entries or software module entries. There may be subsidiary ledgers in which are stored high-volume transactions, such as sales or purchases. Thus, the general ledger is the go-to document for all of the detailed financial accounting information about a business.

If you want to understand the detail for a particular account, such as the current amount of accounts receivable outstanding, you would access the general ledger for this information. In addition, most accounting software packages provide a number of reports that give better insights into the business than just reading through the accounts. In particular, there are aged accounts receivable and aged accounts payable reports that are useful for determining the current list of uncollected accounts receivable and unpaid accounts payable, respectively.

The general ledger is also the source document for the financial statements. There are several financial statements, which are:

- *Income statement.* This report lists the revenues, expenses, and profit or loss of the business for a specific period of time.
- *Balance sheet.* This report lists the assets, liabilities, and equity of the business as of the report date.
- *Statement of cash flows.* This report lists the cash inflows and outflows generated by the business for a specific period of time.

In summary, we have shown that financial accounting involves the recording of business transactions in accounts, which in turn are summarized in the general ledger, which in turn is used to create financial statements. We will now walk through the building blocks of an accounting system, starting with the accounting frameworks from which accounting rules are derived.

Accounting Frameworks

The accounting profession operates under a set of guidelines for how business transactions are to be recorded and reported. There are a multitude of transactions that an organization might enter into, so the corresponding guidelines are also quite large. These guidelines can be subject to a considerable amount of interpretation, so there are standard-setting bodies that maintain and support the guidelines with official pronouncements.

Not every organization operates under the same set of guidelines. There may be different guidelines for different types of entities, and slight differences in guidelines by country. Each of these unique guidelines is referred to as an accounting framework. Once an organization adopts a certain accounting framework, it continues to record transactions and report financial results in accordance with the rules of that framework on a long-term basis. Doing so provides the users of its financial reports with a considerable amount of reporting continuity. Also, because an accounting framework provides a consistent set of rules, anyone reading the financial statements of multiple companies that employ the same framework has a reasonable basis for comparison.

The most commonly-used accounting framework in the United States is GAAP, which is short for Generally Accepted Accounting Principles. GAAP is the most comprehensive accounting framework in the world, with an extensive set of detailed rules covering a massive range of accounting topics. GAAP also provides rules for how to handle accounting transactions in specific industries.

GAAP is derived from the pronouncements of a series of government-sponsored accounting entities, of which the Financial Accounting Standards Board is the latest. The Securities and Exchange Commission also issues accounting pronouncements through its Staff Accounting Bulletins and other announcements that are applicable only to publicly-held companies, and which are considered to be part of GAAP.

International Financial Reporting Standards, or IFRS, is the accounting framework used in most other countries. GAAP is much more rules-based than IFRS, which focuses more on general principles than GAAP. This focus makes the IFRS body of work much smaller, cleaner, and easier to understand than GAAP.

There are several working groups that are gradually reducing the differences between the GAAP and IFRS accounting frameworks, so eventually there should be minor differences in the reported results of a business if it switches between the two frameworks.

The accounting information in this book is based on the GAAP framework.

Accounting Principles

There are a number of accounting principles upon which the accounting frameworks are based. These principles have been derived from common usage, as well as from the documentary efforts of several standard-setting organizations. The principles are:

- *Accrual principle*. The concept that accounting transactions should be recorded in the accounting periods when they actually occur, rather than in the periods when there are cash flows associated with them. This is the foundation of the accrual basis of accounting (as described in a later section). It is important for the construction of financial statements that show what actually happened in an accounting period, rather than being artificially delayed or accelerated by the associated cash flows. For example, if a casino ignores the accrual principle, it records an expense only after paying for it, which might incorporate a lengthy delay caused by the payment terms for the associated supplier invoice.

- *Conservatism principle*. The concept that you should record expenses and liabilities as soon as possible, but record revenues and assets only when certain that they will occur. This introduces a conservative slant to the financial statements that may yield lower reported profits, since revenue and asset recognition may be delayed for some time. This principle tends to encourage the recordation of losses earlier, rather than later. The concept can be taken too far, where a business persistently misstates its results to be worse than is realistically the case.

- *Consistency principle*. The concept that, once a business adopts an accounting principle or method, the company should continue to use it until a demonstrably better principle or method comes along. Not following the consistency principle means that a business could continually jump between different accounting treatments of its transactions that make its long-term financial results extremely difficult to discern.

- *Cost principle*. The concept that a business should only record its assets, liabilities, and equity investments at their original purchase costs. This principle is becoming less valid, as numerous accounting standards are heading in the direction of adjusting to the current fair value of many items.

- *Economic entity principle*. The concept that the transactions of a business should be kept separate from those of its owners and other businesses. This prevents intermingling of assets and liabilities among multiple entities.

- *Full disclosure principle*. The concept that you should include in or alongside the financial statements of a business all of the information that may impact a reader's understanding of those financial statements. The accounting standards

31

have greatly amplified upon this concept in specifying an enormous number of informational disclosures.

- *Going concern principle.* The concept that a business will remain in operation for the foreseeable future. This means that a business would be justified in deferring the recognition of some expenses, such as depreciation, until later periods. Otherwise, the company would have to recognize all expenses at once and not defer any of them.
- *Matching principle.* The concept that, when revenue is recorded, you should record all related expenses at the same time. Thus, a business estimates a bad debt expense at the same time that it records unpaid markers as accounts receivable. This is a cornerstone of the accrual basis of accounting.
- *Materiality principle.* The concept that one should record a transaction in the accounting records if not doing so might have altered the decision making process of someone reading the company's financial statements. This is quite a vague concept that is difficult to quantify, which has led some of the more picayune accountants to record even the smallest transactions.
- *Monetary unit principle.* The concept that a business should only record transactions that can be stated in terms of a unit of currency. Thus, it is easy enough to record the purchase of a fixed asset, since it was bought for a specific price, whereas the value of a casino's system of controls is not recorded. This concept keeps a business from engaging in an excessive level of estimation in deriving the value of its assets and liabilities.
- *Reliability principle.* The concept that only those transactions that can be proven should be recorded. For example, a supplier invoice is solid evidence that an expense has been recorded. This concept is of prime interest to auditors, who are constantly in search of the evidence supporting transactions.
- *Revenue recognition principle.* The concept that one should only recognize revenue when a business has substantially completed the earnings process.
- *Time period principle.* The concept that a business should report the results of its operations over a standard period of time. This may qualify as the most glaringly obvious of all accounting principles, but is intended to create a standard set of comparable periods, which is useful for trend analysis.

It may not initially appear that accounting principles are of much use on a day-to-day basis. However, when there is a question about the proper treatment of a business transaction, it is sometimes useful to resolve the question by viewing the guidance in the relevant accounting framework in light of these accounting principles. Doing so may indicate that one solution more closely adheres to the general intent of the framework, and so is a better solution.

The Accounting Cycle

The accounting cycle is a sequential set of activities used to identify and record an entity's individual transactions. These transactions are then aggregated at the end of each reporting period into financial statements. The accounting cycle is essentially the core recordation activity that an accountant engages in, and is the basis upon which the financial statements are constructed. The following discussion breaks the accounting cycle into the treatment of individual transactions and then closing the books at the end of the accounting period. The accounting cycle for individual transactions is:

1. Identify the event causing an accounting transaction, such as a customer winning a jackpot, paying wages to employees, or buying gaming supplies from suppliers.
2. Prepare the business document associated with the accounting transaction, such as a payout slip, employee check, or supplier check.
3. Identify which accounts are affected by the business document.
4. Record in the appropriate accounts in the accounting database the amounts noted on the business document.

The preceding accounting cycle steps were associated with individual transactions. The following accounting cycle steps are only used at the end of the reporting period, and are associated with the aggregate amounts of the preceding transactions:

5. Prepare a preliminary trial balance, which itemizes the debit and credit totals for each account.
6. Add accrued items, record estimated reserves, and correct errors in the preliminary trial balance with adjusting entries. Examples are the recordation of an expense for supplier invoices that have not yet arrived, and accruing for unpaid wages earned.
7. Prepare an adjusted trial balance, which incorporates the preliminary trial balance and all adjusting entries. It may require several iterations before this report accurately reflects the results of operations of the business.
8. Prepare financial statements from the adjusted trial balance.
9. Close the books for the reporting period.

In the following sections, we expand upon a number of the concepts just noted in the accounting cycle, including accounting transactions, journal entries, ledgers, and the trial balance.

Accounting Transactions

An accounting transaction is a business event having a monetary impact on the financial statements of a business. It is recorded in the accounting records of an organization. Examples of accounting transactions are:

- Winnings at a table game
- Jackpot pay outs to customers
- Receipt of cash to pay off a marker
- Pay gaming taxes to the government
- Purchase fixed assets from a supplier
- Record the depreciation of a fixed asset over time

- Purchase gaming supplies from a supplier
- Borrow funds from a lender
- Issue a dividend to investors
- Sale of assets to a third party

Types of Transaction Cycles

A transaction cycle is an interlocking set of business transactions. Most business transactions can be aggregated into a relatively small number of transaction cycles related to the sale of goods and services, payments to suppliers, payments to employees, and payments to lenders. We explore the nature of these transaction cycles in the following bullet points:

- *Sales cycle.* A casino provides hotel rooms or meals to a customer, issues an invoice, and collects payment. This set of sequential, interrelated activities is known as the sales cycle, or revenue cycle.
- *Purchasing cycle.* A casino issues a purchase order to a supplier for goods, receives the goods, records an account payable, and pays the supplier. There are several ancillary activities, such as the use of petty cash or procurement cards for smaller purchases. This set of sequential, interrelated activities is known as the purchasing cycle, or expenditure cycle.
- *Payroll cycle.* A company records the time of its employees, verifies hours and overtime worked, calculates gross pay, deducts taxes and other with-holdings, and issues paychecks to employees. Other related activities include the payment of withheld income taxes to the government, as well as the issuance of annual W-2 forms to employees. This cluster of activities is known as the payroll cycle.
- *Financing cycle.* A company borrows money from lenders, followed by a series of interest payments and repayments of the debt. Also, it issues stock to investors, in exchange for periodic dividend payments and other payouts if the entity is dissolved. These clusters of transactions are more diverse than the preceding transaction cycles, but may involve substantially more money.

A key role of the accountant is to design an appropriate set of procedures, forms, and integrated controls for each of these transaction cycles, to mitigate the opportunities for fraud and ensure that transactions are processed in as reliable and consistent a manner as possible.

Source Documents

Source documents are the physical basis upon which business transactions are recorded. They usually contain the following information:

- A description of the transaction
- The date of the transaction
- A specific amount of money
- An authorizing signature (in some cases)

Examples of source documents and their related business transactions that appear in the financial records are:

- *Bank statement*. This contains a number of adjustments to a company's book balance of cash on hand that the company should reference to bring its records into alignment with those of a bank.
- *Cash register tape*. This can be used as evidence of cash sales, which supports the recordation of a sale transaction.
- *Credit card receipt*. This can be used as evidence for a disbursement of funds from petty cash.
- *Lockbox check images*. These images support the recordation of cash receipts from customers.
- *Marker*. This describes the amount of credit that a customer has with a casino, and has promised to pay back.
- *Supplier invoice*. This document supports the issuance of a cash, check, or electronic payment to a supplier. A supplier invoice also supports the recordation of an expense, inventory item, or fixed asset.
- *Time card*. This supports the issuance of a paycheck or electronic payment to an employee. If employee hours are being billed to customers, the time card also supports the creation of customer invoices.

Double Entry Accounting

Double entry accounting is a record keeping system under which every transaction is recorded in at least two accounts. There is no upper limit on the number of accounts used in a transaction, but the minimum is two accounts. There are two columns in each account, with debit entries on the left and credit entries on the right. In double entry accounting, the total of all debit entries must match the total of all credit entries. When this happens, a transaction is said to be *in balance*. If the totals do not agree, the transaction is *out of balance*. An out of balance transaction must be corrected before financial statements can be created.

The definitions of a debit and credit are:

- A debit is an accounting entry that either increases an asset or expense account, or decreases a liability or equity account. It is positioned to the left in an accounting entry.
- A credit is an accounting entry that either increases a liability or equity account, or decreases an asset or expense account. It is positioned to the right in an accounting entry.

An account is a separate, detailed record associated with a specific asset, liability, equity, revenue, expense, gain, or loss. Examples of accounts are noted in the following table:

Characteristics of Sample Accounts

Account Name	Account Type	Normal Account Balance
Cash	Asset	Debit
Receivables, casino	Asset	Debit
Fixed assets	Asset	Debit
Accounts payable	Liability	Credit
Accrued liabilities	Liability	Credit
Notes payable	Liability	Credit
Common stock	Equity	Credit
Retained earnings	Equity	Credit
Gaming revenue	Revenue	Credit
Room revenue	Revenue	Credit
Cost of food sales	Expense	Debit
Compensation expense	Expense	Debit
Gaming supplies	Expense	Debit
Utilities expense	Expense	Debit
Travel and entertainment	Expense	Debit
Gain on sale of asset	Gain	Credit
Loss on sale of asset	Loss	Debit

The key point with double entry accounting is that a single transaction always triggers a recordation in *at least* two accounts, as assets and liabilities gradually flow through a business and are converted into revenues, expenses, gains, and losses. We expand upon this concept in the next section.

The Accounting Equation

The *accounting equation* is the basis upon which the double entry accounting system is constructed. In essence, the accounting equation is:

$$Assets = Liabilities + Shareholders' Equity$$

The assets in the accounting equation are the resources that a company has available for its use, such as cash, accounts receivable, and fixed assets. The casino pays for these resources by either incurring liabilities (which is the Liabilities part of the accounting equation) or by obtaining funding from investors (which is the Shareholders' Equity part of the equation). Thus, you have resources with offsetting claims against those resources, either from creditors or investors.

The Liabilities part of the equation is usually comprised of accounts payable that are owed to suppliers, a variety of accrued liabilities, such as sales taxes and income taxes, and debt payable to lenders.

The Shareholders' Equity part of the equation is more complex than simply being the amount paid to the company by investors. It is actually their initial investment, plus any subsequent gains, minus any subsequent losses, minus any dividends or other withdrawals paid to the investors.

This relationship between assets, liabilities, and shareholders' equity appears in the balance sheet, where the total of all assets always equals the sum of the liabilities and shareholders' equity sections.

The reason why the accounting equation is so important is that it is always true - and it forms the basis for all accounting transactions. At a general level, this means that whenever there is a recordable transaction, the choices for recording it all involve keeping the accounting equation in balance.

EXAMPLE

The Creekside Casino engages in the following series of transactions:
1. Creekside sells shares to an investor for $10,000. This increases the cash (asset) account as well as the capital (equity) account.
2. Creekside buys $4,000 of alcoholic beverages from a vendor. This increases the inventory (asset) account as well as the payables (liability) account.
3. Creekside sells the beverages for $6,000. This decreases the inventory (asset) account and creates a cost of goods sold expense that appears as a decrease in the income (equity) account.
4. The sale of Creekside's inventory also creates a sale and offsetting receivable. This increases the receivables (asset) account by $6,000 and increases the income (equity) account by $6,000.
5. Creekside collects cash from the customers to which it sold the beverages. This increases the cash (asset) account by $6,000 and decreases the receivables (asset) account by $6,000.

These transactions appear in the following table:

Item	(Asset) Cash	(Asset) Receivables	(Asset) Inventory		(Liability) Payables	(Equity) Capital	(Equity) Income
(1)	$10,000			=		$10,000	
(2)			$4,000	=	$4,000		
(3)			-4,000	=			-$4,000
(4)		$6,000		=			6,000
(5)	6,000	-6,000		=			
Totals	$16,000	$0	$0	=	$4,000	$10,000	$2,000

37

In the example, note how every transaction is balanced within the accounting equation - either because there are changes on both sides of the equation, or because a transaction cancels itself out on one side of the equation (as was the case when the receivable was converted to cash).

The following table shows how a number of typical accounting transactions are recorded within the framework of the accounting equation:

Transaction Type	Assets	Liabilities + Equity
Buy fixed assets on credit	Fixed assets increase	Accounts payable (liability) increases
Buy inventory on credit	Inventory increases	Accounts payable (liability) increases
Pay dividends	Cash decreases	Retained earnings (equity) decreases
Pay rent	Cash decreases	Income (equity) decreases
Pay supplier invoices	Cash decreases	Accounts payable (liability) decreases
Sell hotel room on credit	Inventory decreases	Income (equity) decreases
Sell hotel room on credit (part 2)	Accounts receivable increases	Income (equity) increases
Sell services on credit	Accounts receivable increases	Income (equity) increases
Sell stock	Cash increases	Equity increases

Here are examples of each of the preceding transactions, where we show how they comply with the accounting equation:

- *Buy fixed assets on credit.* Creekside buys a keno machine on credit for $10,000. This increases the fixed assets (asset) account and increases the accounts payable (liability) account. Thus, the asset and liability sides of the transaction are equal.
- *Buy inventory on credit.* Creekside buys gaming merchandise on credit for $5,000. This increases the inventory (asset) account and increases the accounts payable (liability) account. Thus, the asset and liability sides of the transaction are equal.
- *Pay dividends.* Creekside pays $25,000 in dividends. This reduces the cash (asset) account and reduces the retained earnings (equity) account. Thus, the asset and equity sides of the transaction are equal.
- *Pay rent.* Creekside pays $4,000 in slot machine rent. This reduces the cash (asset) account and reduces the accounts payable (liabilities) account. Thus, the asset and liability sides of the transaction are equal.
- *Pay supplier invoices.* Creekside pays $29,000 on existing supplier invoices. This reduces the cash (asset) account by $29,000 and reduces the accounts payable (liability) account. Thus, the asset and liability sides of the transaction are equal.
- *Sell goods on credit.* Creekside sell beverages to a business conference group for $55,000 on credit. This increases the accounts receivable (asset) account by $55,000, and increases the revenue (equity) account. Thus, the asset and equity sides of the transaction are equal.

- *Sell stock.* Creekside sells $120,000 of its shares to investors. This increases the cash account (asset) by $120,000, and increases the capital stock (equity) account. Thus, the asset and equity sides of the transaction are equal.

Journal Entries

A journal entry is a formalized method for recording a business transaction. It is recorded in the accounting records of a business, usually in the general ledger, but sometimes in a subsidiary ledger that is then summarized and rolled forward into the general ledger (see the Ledger Concept section later in this chapter).

Journal entries are used in a double entry accounting system, where the intent is to record every business transaction in at least two places. For example, when a casino sells merchandise for cash, this increases both the revenue account and the cash account. Or, if merchandise is acquired on account, this increases both the accounts payable account and the inventory account.

The structure of a journal entry is:
- A header line may include a journal entry number and entry date.
- The first column includes the account number and account name into which the entry is recorded. This field is indented if it is for the account being credited.
- The second column contains the debit amount to be entered.
- The third column contains the credit amount to be entered.
- A footer line may also include a brief description of the reason for the entry.

Thus, the basic journal entry format is:

	Debit	Credit
Account name / number	$xx,xxx	
Account name / number		$xx,xxx

The structural rules of a journal entry are that there must be a minimum of two line items in the entry, and that the total amount entered in the debit column equals the total amount entered in the credit column.

A journal entry is usually printed and stored in a binder of accounting transactions, with backup materials attached that justify the entry. This information may be accessed by the company's auditors as part of their annual audit activities.

There are several types of journal entries, including:
- *Adjusting entry.* An adjusting entry is used at month-end to alter the financial statements to bring them into compliance with the relevant accounting framework. For example, a casino could accrue unpaid wages at month-end in order to recognize the wages expense in the current period.

- *Compound entry.* This is a journal entry that includes more than two lines of entries. It is frequently used to record complex transactions, or several transactions at once. For example, the journal entry to record a payroll usually contains many lines, since it involves the recordation of numerous tax liabilities and payroll deductions.
- *Reversing entry.* This is an adjusting entry that is reversed as of the beginning of the following period, usually because an expense was accrued in the preceding period and is no longer needed. Thus, a wage accrual in the preceding period is reversed in the next period, to be replaced by an actual payroll expenditure.

In general, journal entries are not used to record high-volume transactions, such as supplier invoices. These transactions are handled through specialized software modules that present a standard on-line form to be filled out. Once the form is complete, the software automatically creates the accounting record.

The Accruals Concept

An accrual is a journal entry that is used to recognize revenues and expenses that have been earned or consumed, respectively, and for which the related source documents have not yet been received or generated. Accruals are needed to ensure that all revenue and expense elements are recognized within the correct reporting period, irrespective of the timing of related cash flows. Without accruals, the amount of revenue, expense, and profit or loss in a period will not necessarily reflect the actual level of economic activity within a business. Accruals are a key part of the closing process used to create financial statements under the accrual basis of accounting; without accruals, financial statements would be considerably less accurate.

It is most efficient to initially record most accruals as reversing entries. This is a useful feature when a business is expecting to receive an invoice from a supplier in the following period. For example, an accountant may know that a supplier invoice for $20,000 will arrive a few days after the end of a month, but she wants to close the books as soon as possible. Accordingly, she records a $20,000 reversing entry to recognize the expense in the current month. In the next month, the accrual reverses, creating a negative $20,000 expense that is offset by the arrival and recordation of the supplier invoice.

Examples of accruals that a business might record are:

- *Expense accrual for interest.* A local lender issues a loan to a casino, and sends the borrower an invoice each month, detailing the amount of interest owed. The borrower can record the interest expense in advance of invoice receipt by recording accrued interest.
- *Expense accrual for wages.* An employer pays its employees once a month for the hours they have worked through the 26th day of the month. The employer can accrue all additional wages earned from the

27th through the last day of the month, to ensure that the full amount of the wage expense is recognized.

- *Sales accrual.* A casino's hotel operation is compiling room charges for a major government agency, which it is contractually limited to do on a quarterly basis. In the meantime, the hotel can accrue revenue for the amount of services provided to date, even though the charges have not yet been billed.

If a casino records its transactions under the cash basis of accounting, it does not use accruals. Instead, the organization records transactions only when it either pays out or receives cash.

The Chart of Accounts

The chart of accounts defines how accounting information is stored. A properly structured chart of accounts makes it much easier to accumulate and report on information, so the account structure is an area of considerable interest to the accountant. In this section, we give an overview of the chart of accounts and the most common accounts used, and then address the account coding structures for a casino organization.

> **Related Podcast Episode:** Episode 163 of the Accounting Best Practices Podcast discusses the chart of accounts. You can listen to it at: **accounting-tools.com/podcasts** or **iTunes**

The chart of accounts is a listing of all accounts used in the general ledger, usually sorted in order by account number. The accounts are typically numeric, but can also be alphabetic or alphanumeric. The account numbering system is used by the accounting software to aggregate information into an entity's financial statements.

Accounts are usually listed in order of their appearance in the financial statements, starting with the balance sheet and continuing with the income statement. Thus, the chart of accounts begins with cash, proceeds through liabilities and shareholders' equity, and then continues with accounts for revenues and then expenses. Many organizations structure their chart of accounts so that expense information is separately compiled by department; thus, the gaming tables, slot machines, and keno areas could all have the same set of expense accounts.

A five-digit chart of accounts is used by organizations that want to track information at the departmental level. With a five-digit code, they can produce a separate income statement for each department. This format duplicates the account codes found in a three-digit chart of accounts, but then adds a two-digit code to the left, which identifies specific departments. The three-digit codes for expenses (and sometimes also revenues) are then duplicated for each department for which management wants to record information. A sample of the five-digit chart of accounts format follows, using the slot machine and bar departments to show how expense account codes can be duplicated.

Sample Chart of Accounts

Account Number	Department	Description
00-010	xxx	Cash
00-020	xxx	Receivables, casino
00-030	xxx	Receivables, trade
00-040	xxx	Allowance for doubtful accounts
00-050	xxx	Prepaid expenses
00-060	xxx	Food and beverage inventory
00-100	xxx	Fixed assets – Buildings
00-110	xxx	Fixed assets – Computer equipment
00-120	xxx	Fixed assets – Keno equipment
00-130	xxx	Fixed assets – Slot machines
00-140	xxx	Accumulated depreciation
00-200	xxx	Other assets
00-300	xxx	Accounts payable
00-310	xxx	Accrued expenses
00-320	xxx	Current portion of long-term debt
00-330	xxx	Other current liabilities
00-400	xxx	Long-term notes payable
00-500	xxx	Capital stock
00-510	xxx	Retained earnings
10-600	Slots	Revenue – Gaming
20-600	Bar	Revenue – Bar
20-610	Bar	Revenue – Complimentary Beverage Sales
10-802	Slots	Compensation expense
10-810	Slots	Benefits expense
10-815	Slots	Payroll taxes
10-817	Slots	Comps expense
10-822	Slots	Maintenance costs
10-825	Slots	Utilities
10-830	Slots	Other expenses
20-801	Bar	Cost of beverage sales
20-802	Bar	Compensation expense
20-810	Bar	Benefits expense
20-815	Bar	Payroll taxes
20-820	Bar	Licenses
20-825	Bar	Utilities
20-830	Bar	Other expenses

The preceding sample chart of accounts duplicates accounts for each department listed. This is not necessarily the case in reality, since some departments have accounts for which they are the only probable users (such as maintenance in the slot machine department). Thus, some accounts can be avoided by flagging them as inactive in the accounting system. By doing so, they do not appear in the formal chart of accounts.

Major Journal Entries

The following journal entry examples are intended to provide an outline of the general structure of the more common entries encountered. It is impossible to provide a complete set of journal entries that address every variation on every situation, since there are thousands of possible entries.

In each of the following journal entries, we state the topic, the relevant debit and credit, and additional comments as needed.

Revenue journal entries:

- *Hotel and restaurant sales entry*. Debit accounts receivable and credit sales. If a sale is for cash, the debit is to the cash account instead of the accounts receivable account.
- *Allowance for doubtful accounts entry*. Debit bad debt expense and credit the allowance for doubtful accounts. When actual bad debts are identified, debit the allowance account and credit the accounts receivable account, thereby clearing out the associated invoice.

Expense journal entries:

- *Accounts payable entry*. Debit the asset or expense account to which a purchase relates and credit the accounts payable account. When an account payable is paid, debit accounts payable and credit the cash account.
- *Payroll entry*. Debit the wages expense and payroll tax expense accounts, and credit the cash account. There may be additional credits to account for deductions from benefit expense accounts, if employees have permitted deductions for benefits to be taken from their pay.
- *Accrued expense entry*. Debit the applicable expense and credit the accrued expenses liability account. This entry is usually reversed automatically in the following period.
- *Depreciation entry*. Debit depreciation expense and credit accumulated depreciation. These accounts may be categorized by type of fixed asset.

Asset entries:

- *Cash reconciliation entry*. This entry can take many forms, but there is usually a debit to the bank fees account to recognize changes made by the bank, with a credit to the cash account. There may also be a debit to office supplies expense for any check supplies purchased and paid for through the bank account.
- *Prepaid expense adjustment entry*. When recognizing prepaid expenses as expenses, debit the applicable expense account and credit the prepaid expense asset account.
- *Fixed asset addition entry*. Debit the applicable fixed asset account and credit accounts payable.

- *Fixed asset derecognition entry*. Debit accumulated depreciation and credit the applicable fixed asset account. There may also be a gain or loss on the asset derecognition.

Liability entries:

See the preceding accounts payable and accrued expense entries.

Equity entries:

- *Dividend declaration*. Debit the retained earnings account and credit the dividends payable account. Once dividends are paid, this is a debit to the dividends payable account and a credit to the cash account.
- *Stock sale*. Debit the cash account and credit the common stock account.

These journal entry examples are only intended to provide an overview of the general types and formats of accounting entries. There are many variations on the entries presented here that are used to deal with a broad range of business transactions. More detailed journal entries are provided in the following chapters.

The Ledger Concept

A *ledger* is a book or database in which double-entry accounting transactions are stored or summarized. A *subsidiary ledger* is a ledger designed for the storage of specific types of accounting transactions. If a subsidiary ledger is used, the information in it is then summarized and posted to an account in the *general ledger*, which in turn is used to construct the financial statements of a company. The account in the general ledger where this summarized information is stored is called a *control account*. Most accounts in the general ledger are not control accounts; instead, transactions are recorded directly into them.

A subsidiary ledger can be set up to offload data storage for virtually any general ledger account. However, they are usually only created for areas in which there are high transaction volumes, which limits their use to a few areas. Examples of subsidiary ledgers are:
- Accounts receivable ledger
- Fixed assets ledger
- Inventory ledger
- Purchases ledger

> **Tip:** Subsidiary ledgers are used when there is a large amount of transaction information that would clutter up the general ledger. This situation typically arises in companies with significant sales volume. Thus, there may be no need for subsidiary ledgers in a smaller casino.

In order to research accounting information when a subsidiary ledger is used, drill down from the general ledger to the appropriate subsidiary ledger, where the detailed information is stored. Consequently, if you prefer to conduct as much research as possible within the general ledger, use fewer subsidiary ledgers.

Part of the period-end closing process is to post the information in a subsidiary ledger to the general ledger. This is usually a manual step, so verify that all subsidiary ledgers have been appropriately completed and closed before posting their summarized totals to the general ledger. It can be quite a problem if you forget to post the totals from a subsidiary ledger to the general ledger, since that means the resulting financial statements may be missing a batch of crucial transactions.

Tip: If subsidiary ledgers are used, include a step in the closing procedure to post the balances in all subsidiary ledgers to the general ledger, as well as to verify that the subsidiary ledgers have been closed and shifted forward to the next accounting period.

Posting to the General Ledger

Posting refers to the aggregation of financial transactions from where they are stored in subsidiary ledgers, and transferring this information into the general ledger. Information in one of the subsidiary ledgers is aggregated at regular intervals, at which point a summary-level entry is made and posted in the general ledger. In a manual accounting environment, the aggregation may occur at fixed intervals, such as once a day or once a month. For example, if the source ledger were the accounts receivable ledger, the aggregated posting entry might include a debit to the accounts receivable account, and credits to the sales account and various sales tax liability accounts for the sale of merchandise. When posting this entry in the general ledger, a notation could be made in the description field, stating the date range to which the entry applies.

In a computerized accounting environment, posting to the general ledger may be unnoticeable. The software simply does so at regular intervals, or asks if you want to post, and then handles the underlying general ledger posting automatically. It is possible that no posting transaction even appears in the reports generated by the system.

Posting to the general ledger does not occur for lower-volume transactions, which are already recorded in the general ledger. For example, fixed asset purchases may be so infrequent that there is no need for a subsidiary ledger to house these transactions, so they are instead recorded directly in the general ledger.

General Ledger Overview

A general ledger is the master set of accounts in which is summarized all transactions occurring within a business during a specific period of time. The general ledger contains all of the accounts currently being used in a chart of accounts, and is sorted by account number. Either individual transactions or summary-level postings from subsidiary ledgers are listed within each account number, and are sorted by transaction date. Each entry in the general ledger includes a reference number that states the source of the information. The source may be a subsidiary ledger, a journal entry, or a transaction entered directly into the general ledger.

The format of the general ledger varies somewhat, depending on the accounting software being used, but the basic set of information presented for an account within the general ledger is:

- *Transaction number.* The software assigns a unique number to each transaction, so that it can be more easily located in the accounting database if you know the transaction number.
- *Transaction date.* This is the date on which the transaction was entered into the accounting database.
- *Description.* This is a brief description that summarizes the reason for the entry.
- *Source.* Information may be forwarded to the general ledger from a variety of sources, so the report should state the source, in case you need to go back to the source to research the reason for the entry.
- *Debit and credit.* States the amount debited or credited to the account for a specific transaction.

The following sample of a general ledger report shows a possible format that could be used to present information for several transactions that are aggregated under a specific account number.

Sample General Ledger Presentation

Trans. No.	Trans. Date	Description	Source	Debit	Credit
Acct. 10400		**Acct: Accounts Receivable**		**Beginning balance**	**$127,500.00**
10473	3/22/xx	Customer marker	ARL	$8,000.00	
10474	3/23/xx	Customer marker	ARL	4,500.00	
10475	3/24/xx	Credit memo	ARL		1,000.00
10476	3/25/xx	Customer marker	ARL	11,000.00	
18903	3/26/xx	Cash receipt	CRJ		8,000.00
				Ending balance	**$142,000.00**

It is extremely easy to locate information pertinent to an accounting inquiry in the general ledger, which makes it the primary source of accounting information. For example:

- A manager reviews the balance sheet and notices that the amount of debt appears too high. The accountant looks up the debt account in the general ledger and sees that a loan was added at the end of the month.
- A manager reviews the income statement and sees that the bad debt expense for his department is very high. The accountant looks up the expense in the general ledger, drills down to the source journal entry, and sees that a new bad debt projection was the cause of the increase in bad debt expense.

As the examples show, the source of an inquiry is frequently the financial statements; when conducting an investigation, the accountant begins with the general ledger, and may drill down to source documents from there to ascertain the reason(s) for an issue.

The Trial Balance

The trial balance is a report run at the end of an accounting period. It is primarily used to ensure that the total of all debits equals the total of all credits, which means that there are no unbalanced journal entries in the accounting system that would make it impossible to generate accurate financial statements. Printing the trial balance to match debit and credit totals has fallen into disuse, since accounting software rejects the entry of unbalanced journal entries.

The trial balance can also be used to manually compile financial statements, though with the predominant use of computerized accounting systems that create the statements automatically, the report is rarely used for this purpose.

When the trial balance is first printed, it is called the *unadjusted trial balance*. Then, when the accountant corrects any errors found and makes adjustments to bring the financial statements into compliance with the accounting standards, the report is called the *adjusted trial balance*. Finally, after the period has been closed, the report is called the *post-closing trial balance*.

The Trial Balance Format

The initial trial balance report contains the following columns of information:
1. Account number
2. Account name
3. Ending debit balance (if any)
4. Ending credit balance (if any)

Each line item only contains the ending balance in an account, which comes from the general ledger. All accounts having an ending balance are listed in the trial balance; usually, the accounting software automatically blocks all accounts having a zero balance from appearing in the report, which reduces its length. A sample trial balance follows, which employs a compressed account numbering format of just four digits:

Sample Trial Balance

Account Number	Account Description	Unadjusted Trial Balance Debit	Credit
1000	Cash	$60,000	
1500	Accounts receivable	180,000	
2000	Food and beverage inventory	300,000	
3000	Fixed assets	4,210,000	
4000	Accounts payable		$90,000
4500	Accrued liabilities		50,000
4700	Notes payable		420,000
5000	Equity		4,350,000
6000	Revenue		400,000
7200	Cost of food and beverage sales	290,000	
7300	Salaries expense	200,000	
7400	Payroll tax expense	20,000	
7500	Rent expense	35,000	
7600	Other expenses	15,000	
	Totals	$5,310,000	$5,310,000

The adjusted version of a trial balance may combine the debit and credit columns into a single combined column, and add columns to show adjusting entries and a revised ending balance. An adjusting entry is a journal entry that is used at the end of an accounting period to adjust the balances in various general ledger accounts to meet the requirements of accounting standards. This format is useful for revealing the derivation of the line items in financial statements.

The following sample shows adjusting entries. It also combines the debit and credit totals into the second column, so that the summary balance for the total is (and should be) zero. Adjusting entries are added in the next column, yielding an adjusted trial balance in the far right column.

Sample Adjusted Trial Balance

Account Description	Unadjusted Trial Balance	Adjusting Entries	Adjusted Trial Balance
Cash	$60,000		$60,000
Accounts receivable	180,000	$50,000	230,000
Food and beverage inventory	300,000		300,000
Fixed assets (net)	4,210,000		4,210,000
Accounts payable	-90,000		-90,000
Accrued liabilities	-50,000	-25,000	-75,000
Notes payable	-420,000		-420,000
Equity	-4,350,000		-4,350,000
Revenue	-400,000	-50,000	-450,000
Cost of food and beverage sales	290,000		290,000
Salaries expense	200,000	25,000	225,000
Payroll tax expense	20,000		20,000
Rent expense	35,000		35,000
Other expenses	15,000		15,000
Totals	$0	$0	$0

The Extended Trial Balance

An extended trial balance is a standard trial balance to which are added categories extending to the right, and in which are listed the account totals for the balance sheet and the income statement. Thus, all asset, liability, and equity accounts are stated in a balance sheet column, and all revenue, expense, gain, and loss accounts are stated in an income statement column.

The extended trial balance is useful for creating a visual representation of where each of the accounts in the standard trial balance goes in the financial statements, and may be useful for detecting anomalies in the trial balance that should be corrected. A sample of an extended trial balance is shown below. It uses the same trial balance information used to describe the adjusted trial balance format.

Sample Extended Trial Balance

	Unadjusted Trial Balance	Adjusting Entries	Adjusted Trial Balance	Balance Sheet	Income Statement
Cash	$60,000		$60,000	$60,000	
Accounts receivable	180,000	$50,000	230,000	230,000	
Inventory	300,000		300,000	300,000	
Fixed assets (net)	4,210,000		4,210,000	4,210,000	
Accounts payable	-90,000		-90,000	-90,000	
Accrued liabilities	-50,000	-25,000	-75,000	-75,000	
Notes payable	-420,000		-420,000	-420,000	
Equity	-4,350,000		-4,350,000	-4,350,000	
Retained earnings				-135,000	
Revenue	-400,000	-50,000	-450,000		-450,000
Cost of sales	290,000		290,000		290,000
Salaries expense	200,000	25,000	225,000		225,000
Payroll tax expense	20,000		20,000		20,000
Rent expense	35,000		35,000		35,000
Other expenses	15,000		15,000		15,000
Totals	$0	$0	$0	$0	-$135,000

Any computerized accounting system automatically generates financial statements from the trial balance, so the extended trial balance is not a commonly generated report in computerized systems.

Note: The information in the balance sheet and income statement columns in an extended trial balance do not necessarily match the final presentation of these reports, because some of the line items may be aggregated for presentation purposes.

Accrual Basis of Accounting

The accrual basis of accounting is the concept of recording revenues when earned and expenses as incurred. This concept differs from the cash basis of accounting, under which revenues are recorded when cash is received, and expenses are recorded when cash is paid. For example, a casino operating under the accrual basis of accounting will record an expense as incurred, while a cash basis casino would instead wait to pay its supplier before recording the expense.

The accrual basis of accounting is advocated under both the GAAP and IFRS accounting frameworks. Both of these frameworks provide guidance regarding how to account for revenue and expense transactions in the absence of the cash receipts or payments that would trigger the recordation of a transaction under the cash basis of accounting.

The accrual basis tends to provide more even recognition of revenues and expenses over time than the cash basis, and so is considered by investors to be the most valid accounting system for ascertaining the results of operations, financial position, and cash flows of a business. In particular, it supports the matching principle, under which revenues and all related expenses are to be recorded within the same reporting period; by doing so, it should be possible to see the full extent of the profits and losses associated with specific business transactions within a single reporting period.

The accrual basis requires the use of estimated reserves in certain areas. For example, a company should recognize an expense for estimated bad debts that have not yet been incurred. By doing so, all expenses related to a revenue transaction are recorded at the same time as the revenue, which results in an income statement that fully reflects the results of operations. These estimates may not be entirely accurate, and so can lead to materially inaccurate financial statements. Consequently, a considerable amount of care must be used when estimating reserves.

A significant failing of the accrual basis is that it can indicate the presence of profits, even though the associated cash inflows have not yet occurred. The result can be a supposedly profitable casino that is starved for cash, and which may therefore go bankrupt despite its reported level of profitability.

Summary

The main focus of this chapter was to reveal how business transactions are recorded in the accounting database. The level of detail given was intended to provide the reader with a basic understanding of the process flow, where transactions are summarized into accounts. We also defined a number of key concepts, including accounts, journal entries, the chart of accounts, and ledgers. In the next chapter, we turn to accounting issues that are specific to the gaming industry.

Chapter 3
Gaming-Specific Accounting

Introduction

There are a number of accounting transactions within the gaming industry that are rarely found elsewhere. For example, one must account for gaming win, comps, chips, delayed bets, unpaid winners, incentive programs, promotional allowances, jackpot insurance, and point redemptions. We cover all of these topics in the following sections. The sequence followed is to begin with revenue and jackpots, then marketing topics, and then general topics and issues related to specific functional areas.

Revenue Recognition

Revenue is the win from gaming operations, which is the difference between gaming wins and losses. Revenue is *not* the total amount wagered by customers. The Nevada Gaming Control Board provides detailed definitions of what constitutes gross revenue in its Regulation 6, which covers accounting regulations. For example, here is their definition of gross revenue for a table game:

> For each table game, gross revenue equals the closing table game bankroll plus credit slips for cash, chips, tokens, or personal/payroll checks returned to the casino cage, plus drop, less opening table game bankroll, fills to the table, and money transfers issued from the game through the use of a cashless wagering system.

Regulation 6 goes on to provide the following definition of gross revenue for a slot machine:

> For each slot machine, or gaming device, gross revenue equals drop less fills to the machine or gaming device and jackpot payouts, and includes all money received by the licensee from a patron to play a slot machine or gaming device. Additionally, the initial hopper load is not a fill and does not affect gross revenue. The difference between the initial hopper load and the total amount that is in the hopper at the end of the licensee's fiscal year must be adjusted accordingly as an addition to or subtraction from the drop for that year.

Gross gaming revenue is not reported on a gaming entity's external financial statements, only its *net* gaming revenue. Gross gaming revenue may be reported internally.

Several additional considerations are:

- *Participating slot machines*. Slot machines may be leased, with terms that require a casino to pay a participating fee to the lessor. If so, the full amount of the win is still recorded by the casino as revenue, while the participating fee is recognized as an expense.

- *Promotional allowances.* Casinos routinely give their customers free goods and services, such as complimentary rooms, meals, and entertainment. These comps are used to induce customers to gamble within the casino. It is acceptable to add the retail value of comps to gross revenue and then deduct this amount to arrive at net revenue.

Deferred Revenue

Revenues generated by the race and sports book area are unique in a casino, in that they can result in deferred revenue. This is the case when bets are placed on events that have yet to occur. When cash related to future events is received, the accounting department debits cash and credits a deferred revenue liability account. Once the underlying events occur, this liability is debited to flush it out of the accounting system, while the applicable revenue account is credited to recognize the revenue.

Breakage

When a customer is a member of a slot club, the computer system will probably be configured to grant a certain number of points as the person continues to play, such as issuing one point for every dollar spent. These points can be used for additional gambling on the slot machines, or to purchase merchandise or meals at the casino. It may also be possible to convert the points into cash. For example, a person could play the slots all morning and then go to the in-house restaurant, hand over his player card, and be served a meal for free.

What if the customer does not redeem accrued points? The unexercised amount of these points is referred to as *breakage*. The amount of breakage associated with unredeemed points should be recognized as revenue. The question is, when should the recognition occur? If there is a historical pattern of how customers redeem points, the casino can estimate the amount of breakage likely to occur, and recognize it in proportion to the historical redemption pattern.

No revenue related to breakage should be recognized if it is probable that such recognition will result in a significant revenue reversal at a later date.

Track Fees

The racing operation of a casino may receive a video feed from a racing track for races on which the casino is offering betting activity. The resulting bets are usually forwarded to the racing track (or *track entity*) that is providing the video feed, for inclusion in the bets taken at the track. The casino earns a commission from the track entity for forwarding these wagers. Offsetting the commission is a fee charged to the casino by the track entity. This fee is essentially a reduction of the commission being paid to the casino, so the two items are netted for accounting purposes.

Discounts on Losses

Casinos may offer discounts on losses to top-level players, which is used to attract more high-volume business. Under this arrangement, a customer only has to pay a discounted amount of any losses (such as a 5% reduction) as of the end of the person's visit. Conversely, if the customer experienced net winnings during a visit, he still receives the full amount of any winnings. These discounts reduce the amount of revenue recognized by a casino.

EXAMPLE

A casino offers a high roller a 5% discount in his losses, as long as he engages in a certain amount of playing time during his visit. By the end of his visit, the customer has lost $500,000, which is revenue for the casino. However, the 5% discount is a reduction of $25,000 in the amount of the loss, so the actual revenue that the casino can recognize is $475,000.

Accounting for Jackpots

A casino must accrue a liability for a jackpot won by a customer as soon as there is an obligation to pay. A liability is recorded for slot machines that contain a base (minimum) jackpot. However, it is not necessary to recognize this liability when a slot machine is taken out of service. Thus, the existence of a base jackpot only triggers a liability when there is an obligation to pay the jackpot.

A slot machine may feature a *progressive jackpot*, in which the amount of the jackpot increases for every game played. Once someone wins the jackpot, the amount resets to a lower level. In some gaming jurisdictions, the incremental portion of this jackpot is considered to be funded by customers, and the assumption is that it will eventually be paid out. In this situation, the incremental amount of the jackpot should be accrued as a liability at the time of play, since customers are considered to be funding the jackpot at this time. The casino is merely holding the funds in escrow until a payout occurs.

A variation on the progressive jackpot is the *linked progressive*, where a number of slot machines share a progressive meter, so that the meter on all of the machines increases when money is fed into any one of them. The result can be extremely large jackpots. The accounting is the same as for a normal progressive jackpot.

Another variation on the progressive jackpot is the *wide area progressive*, where a third party (such as the slot machine manufacturer) operates the system at multiple locations. In this case, the third party is responsible for jackpots, not the casino. The third party charges a fee to participating casinos in exchange for managing the system.

A casino may set aside slot machines that offer free play for certain non-cash prizes. Any prizes awarded from these machines are considered a promotional expense. They do not impact the revenue reported by a casino in any way.

Jackpot Insurance

As a risk management measure, a casino may elect to acquire insurance against the risk of losses on large jackpots. Under this arrangement, the casino pays a premium to a third party insurer to reimburse it if a large jackpot is paid out, usually for a specific type of game. The casino uses this insurance to eliminate the probability of a large cash outflow. Instead, the casino incurs a more consistent cash flow, one that is reduced by the amount of the insurance premium in each period.

When a casino has a claim under a jackpot insurance policy, the recovery is reported as net gaming revenue. Jackpot insurance premiums are included in the calculation of net gaming revenue (as a deduction).

If an insurance premium is paid in advance, the amount is to be amortized over the term of the policy. If the amount of insurance coverage over the term of the policy varies, then recognize the premium in proportion to the amount of coverage provided in each period.

Accounting for Unpaid Winners

A winner of a keno or race and sports bet may not come forward with a winning ticket, in which case no winnings are paid out. In this situation, the amounts owed to unpaid winners are considered a liability of the casino.

Management can set a policy for the period within which tickets must be submitted for pay outs. Once the designated period has ended, the casino does not have an obligation to pay a winner, which therefore terminates the unpaid winnings liability.

Loyalty and Incentive Programs

Casinos have multi-layered marketing and reward programs that are designed to both pull in new customers and reward existing ones for their loyalty. The accounting for these programs can vary, depending on their nature. The main factors to consider are whether program benefits are discretionary or nondiscretionary, as noted in the following sub-sections.

Discretionary Incentives

A program is discretionary when there is no obligation by the casino to offer additional rewards to a customer. These expenditures are usually intended to foster new play by customers that will generate incremental additional revenue for the casino. When discretionary expenditures are linked to the occurrence of future revenues, the cost of the incentive can be recognized at the later of:

- The date when the related revenue is recognized by the casino; or
- The date when the incentive is offered.

EXAMPLES

A casino offers a free meal to anyone who plays the $1 slots for at least two hours. The free meal is triggered after the revenue generating event, but the two actions are so close together in time that the revenue and related expense recognition are essentially on the same date.

A casino offers a customer $1,000 of airfare reimbursement, on the condition that he then play for at least two days in the casino. Reimbursement occurs when the customer checks out of the casino on the last day of his trip. The reimbursement expense is recognized immediately after the related gaming revenue from the customer is recognized.

In effect, a casino will not incur this type of expense unless the related revenue is also recognized.

Nondiscretionary Incentives – Cash Redemption Allowed

Nondiscretionary incentives are issued based on the past actions of a customer. These types of incentives primarily relate to slot clubs, where customers earn points as they play. The points can then be redeemed for free play, merchandise, meals, and so forth. The most theoretically correct way to account for these nondiscretionary incentives is to allocate a portion of the revenue generated by the underlying transaction (such as paying $5 at a $5 slot machine) to the incentive (the points generated by paying the $5), based on relative fair values. The revenue allocated to the incentive is deferred until such time as it is redeemed.

EXAMPLE

A customer is playing the $1 slots, and pays a total of $200 into the machine. The casino's incentive policy is to issue 10 points for every $1 paid into the machine, which means that the customer has earned 2,000 points. The cash redemption value of a point is $0.01, so the total cash redemption value is $20. The $200 paid in is then allocated between the gaming win and the points in the following manner:

$200 total cash in - $20 cash redemption value = $180 revenue that can be recognized immediately

The casino accrues a cash benefit liability for the $20 award. The customer later redeems the award for cash, at which time the casino debits the liability and credits cash.

In many cases, customers redeem their points immediately after earning them, so there is no delay in revenue recognition.

Nondiscretionary Incentives – Free Play Only

When a nondiscretionary incentive is given to customers and it can only be used for free play, it is more difficult to determine the value of the incentive. There is no cash redemption, so instead we compare the fair values of the cash paid in by the customer and the amount of free play granted to him. The following example illustrates the concept.

EXAMPLE

A customer plays a slot machine for hours. He plays an aggregate of $10,000, receives $9,300 in cash payouts (an implied hold percentage by the casino of 7%), and also receives $200 of free play. The transaction is therefore comprised of the $10,000 played and the $200 of free play, or $10,200 of total value. The amount of revenue to be deferred is:

$$\$200 \text{ free play} \div (\$10,000 \text{ played} + \$200 \text{ free play}) = 0.02$$

$$\$10,000 \times 0.02 = \$200$$

The amount of revenue the casino would record without the free play benefit would have been $700, which is the net of the cash received and paid out. However, the revenue deferral (a debit) is $200, so the net revenue recognized in the period is $500.

In the following period, the customer uses his $200 of free play. Assuming that the implied hold percentage of 7% holds true, there will be a 93% payout to the customer, which is a $186 debit to gaming revenue. In addition, the initial $200 revenue deferral will be reversed. The next effect is:

+	$700	Initial revenue recognition by casino
-	200	Revenue deferral in first reporting period
=	500	Revenue recognized in first reporting period
+	200	Reversal of revenue deferral in second reporting period
-	186	Payout to customer in second reporting period
=	$514	Cumulative revenue recognition

The example shows that the extension of free play to a customer will likely result in a large proportion of the free play being paid out, resulting in a much lower revenue level by the casino than would otherwise be the case.

Nondiscretionary Incentives – Multiple Redemption Options

Incentives may be provided to customers that have multiple redemption options. If so, the casino should record the associated liability based on its history of how customers normally redeem the incentives. If there is no way to do this, instead assume that customers will choose the redemption option that has the highest cost to the casino. This means that a cash redemption option is the most likely option taken, usually followed by free play. Redemptions for meals, rooms, or merchandise have a lower cost to the casino, and so are the least likely alternative.

Reporting Considerations

The preceding discussion of liabilities associated with loyalty and incentive programs is highly relevant to the issuance of financial statements, since this liability should be reported in the balance sheet. Whenever a casino intends to issue its financial statements to outside parties, it should follow a procedure for estimating these liabilities. In particular, be aware that the year-end audit will likely include an audit of how these liabilities were calculated.

Promotional Allowances

The most successful gaming establishments are aggressive marketers. They routinely issue mailings regarding special events, as well as coupons, vouchers, and so forth. They may also purchase mailing lists of people whose demographic and income profiles make them good candidates for gaming activities. They also host special events, such as slot machine or games tournaments, with prizes. They also ask their best customers to bring along friends who may become patrons, usually offering discounts or comps to attract these new people. All of these costs are charged to expense as incurred.

A gaming organization may have no intention of earning a profit from a tournament, where there is no entry fee and no banked games, and where any prizes given are not funded by the tournament participants. In these situations, the cost to the gaming organization is considered a marketing expense.

Another type of promotional allowance is the *cash-deposit incentive*, which is an automatic percentage increase in the amount of cash that a player deposits in the cage. This award is now the player's money, irrespective of further actions by the player. Consequently, it is treated as an up-front promotional expense.

Yet another incentive is *walk-in money*, which is a cash payment to a high roller in exchange for that person agreeing to play at the casino. This is an up-front payment, and is not subsequently reduced if the player plays a minimal amount. Consequently, it is also considered an up-front promotional expense.

Customers may be offered a percentage discount if they pay their outstanding credit within a specific period of time. This is essentially an early payment discount, and reduces the amount of net revenue recognized.

Advertising

Advertising is the promotion of a business or its products, with the intent of creating a positive image or stimulating customer purchases. The costs incurred for advertising can be aggregated into two areas, which are the production of advertisements and their dissemination. The accounting for advertising costs is as follows:

- *Production costs*. Charge advertising production costs to expense as incurred or when the related advertising first takes place.

- *Dissemination costs.* Charge advertising costs to expense as used. For example, charge the cost to air a television advertisement to expense as the airtime is used.

This treatment is based on the belief that the beneficial effects of advertising are short-lived, and because it is difficult to determine the number of periods over which the resulting benefits can be measured.

> **Tip:** Sales materials can be accounted for as prepaid supplies, which spreads recognition of the related expense over the usage period until the on-hand supply is used up.

Gaming Chips and Tokens

A casino may maintain a large stock of chips and tokens that it exchanges with customers for their cash or markers. When a casino buys chips and tokens, it has two possible methods of accounting for them, which are:

- *Immediate write off.* If the acquisition cost is relatively low, it may be easier to charge the cost to expense as incurred.
- *Capitalization.* If the acquisition cost is relatively high, it is acceptable to record the chips and tokens as assets and depreciate them over the useful lives of the items.

A casino places a certain number of chips in service, which is closely monitored. If the number of chips in the custody of the casino is lower than the number of chips placed in service, the difference represents a liability for the casino, since the missing chips are held by customers who may redeem them. The following accounting issues are associated with this liability:

- *Missing chips.* Some chips will never be redeemed, either because they have been lost or because customers prefer to keep them as souvenirs. The accounting staff regularly eliminates part of the liability based on an estimate of how many chips will never be redeemed. The offsetting entry when the liability is reduced is an increase in net gaming revenue. Nonetheless, there is a real redemption liability that may require a cash payout at some point in the future.
- *Discontinued chips.* Management may decide to stop using certain denominations or themes of gaming chips. If the casino gives proper public notice under the applicable gaming regulations, it will no longer have a liability for any remaining chips that are outstanding, and so can reverse any remaining liability associated with those chips.

Licensing and Preopening Costs

A casino may have a number of startup costs, of which the most important is the cost incurred to obtain a gaming license. In this section, we address the accounting for this license, and other startup costs.

Gaming License Costs

A casino cannot offer gaming to the public until it has obtained a gaming license from the applicable government. This may require lobbying fees, legal advice, and similar charges. These costs should be charged to expense until such time as it becomes likely that a gaming license will be granted. Once the grant is probable, one-time costs incurred between that date and the grant of the license in order to obtain the license can be capitalized into an intangible asset. Internal costs (such as staff time) are not included in this asset.

If the gaming license asset has a finite life (such as the term of the license), then amortize the asset over that period. The default amortization method is the straight-line method, though an alternative can be used if there is a different pattern in which the economic benefits of the asset are being consumed.

In some gaming jurisdictions, the renewal requirements for a gaming license are so minor that there is realistically no way that the license will not be renewed. Or, there is no history of the gaming commission revoking a license that has already been granted, so there is a reasonable assumption that a casino's license will be continued into the future. If so, it is assumed that the gaming license has an indefinite life, and so it is not amortized at all. However, this state of affairs should be reviewed periodically to see if the useful life of the asset is no longer indefinite. If so, begin amortizing it over the estimated useful life.

When an asset has an indefinite life, it must be evaluated for impairment at least annually, to see if its fair value has declined below its carrying amount, and the difference is not recoverable. If so, write down the book value to match the fair value. A more frequent impairment analysis may be warranted if there is an event or a change in circumstances that makes it more likely than not that the asset is impaired.

The carrying amount of the asset is not recoverable if it exceeds the sum of the undiscounted cash flows expected to result from the use of the asset over its remaining useful life and its final disposition. These cash flow estimates should incorporate assumptions that are reasonable in relation to the assumptions the entity uses for its budgets, forecasts, and so forth. If there are a range of possible cash flow outcomes, consider using a probability-weighted cash flow analysis.

The amount of an impairment loss is the difference between an asset's carrying amount and its fair value. Once an impairment loss is recognized, this reduces the carrying amount of the asset, so it may be necessary to alter the amount of periodic amortization being charged against the asset to adjust for this lower carrying amount (otherwise, an excessively large amortization expense will be incurred over the remaining useful life of the asset).

Only test for the recoverability of an asset when the circumstances indicate that its carrying amount may not be recoverable. Examples of such situations are:

- *Cash flow*. There are historical and projected operating or cash flow losses associated with the asset.
- *Disposal*. The asset is more than 50% likely to be sold or otherwise disposed of significantly before the end of its previously estimated useful life.
- *Legal*. There is a significant adverse change in legal factors or the business climate that could affect the asset's value.
- *Market price*. There is a significant decrease in the asset's market price.

Preopening Costs

Preopening activities are those activities required to bring a casino facility into a condition ready for its operation. Essentially, the accounting for preopening costs is to expense them as incurred. Examples of these costs are:

- Compensation for employees directly associated with the opening
- Consulting costs related to the opening
- Employee relocation costs
- Employee training
- Marketing costs related to the opening
- Operating costs incurred between the completion of construction and the start of operations
- Recruiting costs

Preopening expenses may be recorded on the income statement as a separate line item. If these costs are not reported on a separate line item, then they may instead be described in the accompanying footnote disclosures.

Tax Impact of Customer Credit

The top-level players in a casino usually play on credit. Given the large amounts of wagering involved, it may be some time before the full amount of an outstanding credit has been collected. Depending on the taxing jurisdiction, a casino may be allowed to pay its monthly gaming tax based on the amount of cash received during the period, which effectively defers the recognition of outstanding credits granted for tax purposes.

Deferred Income Taxes

A casino is likely to experience a deferred income tax liability under the following circumstances:

- Receivables are recognized under the accrual basis of accounting for financial statement reporting, and using the when-collected method for income tax reporting (see the preceding Tax Impact of Customer Credit section).

- The recognition of costs as expenses is deferred under the accrual basis of accounting, but is recognized when paid for income tax reporting.
- Jackpots for progressive slots are accrued based on meter readings for financial statement reporting, but are recognized for income tax reporting purposes when paid.

Cocktail Service

A casino usually provides free cocktails to its players, to encourage them to continue playing. As long as they remain at a gaming table or slot machine, they will be served free drinks. To this end, cocktail servers rotate through the casino floor, taking orders and delivering drinks. By doing so, players do not need to leave their gaming seats to obtain a drink.

When a cocktail server places a drink order with the bartender, the server also tells the bartender which department should be charged for the cost of the drink (such as the gaming pit or slots). By assigning drink costs to specific parts of the casino floor, an analyst can subtract these costs from the profits generated by each part of the casino, resulting in a more accurate view of the true profitability of each profit-generating segment.

If a customer is not playing at a gaming table or slot machine, then they must pay for drinks. In this case, the server keeps a drinks ticket open until payment is received. These payments are then rung up in the computer system.

A sample journal entry that documents these transactions is shown next.

	Debit	Credit
Cash	$420	
Receivables - MasterCard	180	
Receivables - Visa	210	
Comp Expense – Pit	590	
Comp Expense - Slots	700	
Revenue - Food		$130
Revenue - Alcohol		1,720
Tip (liability)		250
Cocktail server #EM4221deposit, on 12/05/20X1		

The preceding sample entry summarizes the following events:
- The server issues complimentary drinks valued at $1,290 to players
- The server also received cash and credit card payments for an additional $810 related to food and drink purchases, as well as tips
- The total revenue recorded is $1,850

Transfer Pricing

When customers receive complimentary drinks, meals, rooms, and so forth, how does this impact the reporting of financial results for a casino? The most common case is someone gambling on the casino floor who is provided with free drinks. The drinks are provided by the bar, which is a separate profit center from the gambling operations. If the bar were to simply give away these drinks, it would record an enormous cost of drinks, and therefore a resounding loss.

To avoid this situation and show the true profitability of the bar, it is necessary for the bar to record the normal retail price of each drink that is being comped to a customer. This retail price is then charged to the profit center where the drinks are being consumed, which is any of the locations on the casino floor, such as the slots and table games. The ultimate outcome is profit center financial statements that accurately portray profits and losses. This transfer of the drink price is known as *transfer pricing*.

Many types of comps are handed out by the casino host department, which handles relations between registered customers and the casino. If a customer has generated a substantial amount of earnings for the casino, then he will receive more comps from his assigned casino host. Since the casino host department is responsible for issuing these comps, the retail price of the comps should be charged back to that department, which is then considered a marketing cost of the casino.

Each profit center should be assigned at least one comps expense line item in the chart of accounts, so that these transfer prices can be clearly delineated in the profit center financial statements.

Coin Booth

One or more coin booths may be situated in or near the slot machines. Their purpose is to make change for customers who want to convert bills into coins or tokens. A coin booth fulfills the same function for coin clerks, who roam the slot machine area and conduct on-the-spot bill conversions for customers. A coin booth may also disburse jackpots to customers if the hopper on a slot machine does not have a sufficient number of coins to pay out a jackpot.

The accounting for a coin booth is relatively simple – it is just like a very well-funded petty cash box. Instead of having a few hundred dollars, as a petty cash box contains, a coin booth may hold several tens of thousands of dollars. At any time, the amount of cash and receipts for paid out amounts should equal the imprest balance that is assigned to a coin booth. For example, a coin booth has an imprest balance of $30,000. During the course of a day, the booth disburses $10,000 of coins to customers and coin clerks in exchange for bills. It also pays out $5,000 in jackpots to customers who present proper evidence of having won jackpots (such as a jackpot payout ticket). At the end of the day, the coin booth swaps the $10,000 of bills with the cage for $10,000 of coins, and also swaps its jackpot receipts for $5,000 of currency. Thus, by the end of the day, the coin booth has returned to its original funding balance.

Both the coin booth cashier and the cage cashier on either side of these swap transactions must sign the forms describing the amount of the funds transferred.

At the end of each shift, the outgoing cashier prepares a cash balance report that summarizes the ending balance of cash and receipts on hand. The incoming cashier verifies the amounts on this report, and then signs it to take responsibility for the cash.

Drop Accounting

Once all hard counts and soft counts have been completed in the count rooms at the end of each shift or game day, the resulting summary reports are used as the basis for an accounting entry. The following is an example of the entry for one of the gaming tables.

	Debit	Credit
Cash	$7,500	
Paid Outs	2,400	
Caribbean Stud Poker Drop		$7,500
Cage Reserves		2,400
Drop recorded for table 10 in Pit 1, on 12/05/20X1		

The preceding sample entry summarizes the following events:
- The dealer accepted $7,500 cash from players, exchanging them for chips. The players then used the chips to place bets, which represent revenue to the casino. The revenue is described in the "Caribbean Stud Poker Drop" line item.
- The decline in cage reserves represents a transfer of chips worth $2,400 from the cage to the table. The fill is assumed to be the same as the paid outs to players when they win.

Summary

Casinos are supposed to operate under the accrual basis of accounting. However, a quick perusal of the Gaming Operations chapter will reveal that most revenue-related activities are conducted on an all-cash basis. The result is likely to be a minimal difference between cash-basis and accrual accounting in this area. However, there is a definite need for accruals in other areas. In particular, a liability should be recognized for outstanding chips and tokens that could last for several years. There may also be liabilities for unpaid winners, as well as for unused points.

Another significant accounting area is the use of transfer pricing to charge comps back to those profit centers that are benefiting from free items being given to customers. There should be a well-established system in place for setting transfer prices, charging them to profit centers, and backing the resulting intercompany revenue out of the gross sales figure for financial reporting purposes.

Chapter 4
Payroll Accounting

Introduction

One of the primary responsibilities of the casino accountant is to process payroll, since the typical casino employs a relatively large number of staff in comparison to other industries. This chapter contains the essentials of payroll accounting activities, covering the following topics:

- Employee time tracking
- Gross pay calculations
- Types of payroll taxes
- Income tax withholdings
- Benefits and other deductions
- Net pay
- Remitting payroll taxes
- Payments to employees
- The payroll register
- Payroll journal entries

The ordering of these topics approximates the flow of transactions for the processing of payroll, from the initial collection of time worked information, through the determination of gross pay, and concluding with net pay, payments to employees, and the recordation of payroll.

Related Podcast Episodes: Episodes 126-129 of the Accounting Best Practices Podcast discuss the payroll system. They are available at: **accounting-tools.com/podcasts** or **iTunes**

Employee Time Tracking

In order to pay hourly employees, it is necessary to have a system in place for tracking their hours worked. A tracking system may involve the use of a timecard. A timecard is usually printed on heavier-weight paper and is stored in a central timecard rack. Employees can fill it out by hand, or they can insert it into a punch clock, which stamps the time on it. There are separate columns for the beginning and ending times when regular hours and overtime hours are worked. There is also a small block next to each day of regular and overtime hours, in which the accountant enters the total time worked for that day. These daily totals are then accumulated into overtime and regular time totals at the bottom of the timecard. Both the employee and his or her supervisor should sign the card. A sample timecard appears in the next exhibit.

Sample Timecard

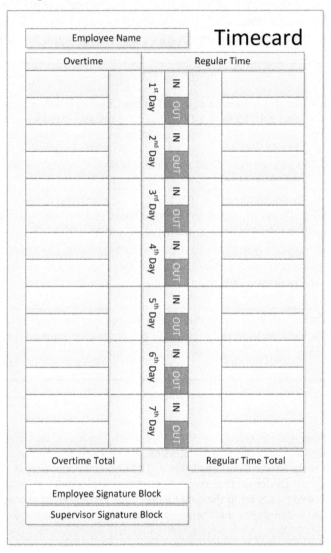

Gross Pay Calculations

Gross pay is the amount of compensation to be paid to an employee before any deductions are withheld from the pay. Though not especially difficult to calculate, there are some issues to consider when deriving gross pay, which are dealt with in the following sub-sections.

Hourly Rate Plan

The simplest and most commonly-used method for determining the compensation of an hourly employee is the hourly rate plan, under which hours worked are multiplied by an employee's hourly rate. This method can be more complicated if there is a shift differential or overtime. A shift differential is extra pay earned by employees who work a less than desirable shift, such as the evening, night, or weekend shifts.

EXAMPLE

Arlo Montaigne works the night shift as a chef at the Chief's Casino. He earns a base wage of $13.50 per hour, plus a $0.50 shift differential. In the most recent work week, he logs 39 hours of work. The calculation of his wages earned under the hourly rate plan is:

($13.50 base wage + $0.50 shift differential) × 39 hours = $546.00

If there is a shift differential, add it to the base wage prior to calculating overtime.

What if an employee works a fraction of an hour? A computerized payroll system automatically converts this to a fraction of an hour. However, an accountant that manually calculates wages may use a variety of simplification methods, such as rounding up to the nearest quarter-hour.

> **Tip:** If a calculation simplification method is being used for determining fractions of hours worked, be sure to state the method in the employee manual, preferably with a sample calculation. This reduces any employee uncertainty about how their pay is calculated.

EXAMPLE

The Nickel 'n Dime Casino calculates wages for its employees by hand. In the most recent week, dealer Mortimer Davis worked 39 hours and 41 minutes. The Nickel bookkeeper could use a calculator to determine that 41 minutes is 0.6833 hours (calculated as 41 minutes ÷ 60 minutes) and pay the dealer on that basis. However, prior calculation errors have led to a company policy of rounding up to the next quarter hour. Accordingly, the accountant rounds the 41 minutes up to 45 minutes, and therefore records 39 ¾ hours for Mr. Davis.

Overtime

Overtime is a 50% multiplier that is added to an employee's base wage for hours worked over 40 hours in a work week. This calculation is subject to some variation by state, so review local regulations to see if there is an overriding overtime calculation in place. Here are two rules to consider when calculating overtime pay:
- Do not include in the 40 base hours such special hours as holidays, jury duty, sick time, or vacations.

- Add the shift differential (the extra amount paid to someone working a late shift) to the base wage, and then calculate overtime based on this combined figure.

EXAMPLE

Alfredo Montoya works the evening shift at a casino, which adds $1 of shift differential per hour to his base wage of $15 per hour. In the most recent work week, he worked 50 hours. The overtime premium he will be paid is based on the combined $16 wage that includes his shift differential. Thus, his overtime rate is $8 per hour. The calculation of his total compensation for that week is:

50 hours × aggregate base pay of $16/hour	=	$800
10 hours × overtime premium of $8/hour	=	<u>80</u>
Total compensation	=	<u>$880</u>

EXAMPLE

Alfredo Montoya works 35 hours during a week that includes Memorial Day. His employer will pay him for a 43-hour work week, which adds the eight hours of the federal holiday to his hours worked. However, this will not include any overtime pay, since only 35 hours were actually worked.

There may be situations where an employee is paid different rates at different times during the work period. This situation may arise when the individual works on different jobs that have differing rates of pay associated with them. In these cases, there are three possible options for calculating overtime, which are:
- Base the overtime rate on the highest wage rate paid during the period
- Base the overtime rate on the average wage rate paid during the period
- Base the overtime rate on the wage rate paid after the 40th hour

The last alternative for calculating overtime requires the prior approval of the affected employee.

EXAMPLE

Marcel Moheko worked on two maintenance jobs at a casino during the past work week. He worked on Job A for 30 hours, and was paid $20.00 per hour while working on that job. He worked 15 hours on Job B, and was paid $25.00 per hour for that job. The last job on which he worked was Job A. The calculation of his overtime pay under the three calculation methods is:

	Based on Highest Rate	Based on Average Rate	Based on Last Rate
Job A pay rate	$20.00	$20.00	$20.00
Job B pay rate	$25.00	$25.00	$25.00
Weighted average pay rate*	$21.25	$21.25	$21.25
Overtime rate	$12.50	$10.63	$10.00
Overtime hours	5	5	5
Total overtime paid	$62.50	$53.15	$50.00

* Calculated as ($20.00 × 75%) + ($25.00 × 25%)

Tips

In general, any tips that employees receive from customers are treated as taxable income. Employees are required to report cash tips to the company by the tenth day of the month after the month in which they received the tips, but not if the tips received were less than $20. This report should include:

- Tips forwarded by the company to employees that were paid with charge cards
- Tips employees received directly from customers
- Tips distributed from a tip-sharing arrangement

Employees report tips to the company on Form 4070, Employee's Report of Tips to Employer. A sample of the form is noted next. It is also allowable to create a similar form or an electronic system for employees to use. Such forms or systems must contain exactly the same information that would otherwise be reported on Form 4070, as well as the employee's signature (an electronic signature is acceptable if an electronic reporting system is used). Any electronic system must be capable of producing a hard copy, in case the IRS audits tip income.

Sample IRS Form 4070

Form **4070** (Rev. August 2005) Department of the Treasury Internal Revenue Service	**Employee's Report of Tips to Employer**		OMB No. 1545-0074
Employee's name and address		Social security number	
Employer's name and address (include establishment name, if different)		1 Cash tips received	
		2 Credit and debit card tips received	
		3 Tips paid out	
Month or shorter period in which tips were received from , to ,		4 Net tips (lines 1 + 2 - 3)	
Signature		Date	
For Paperwork Reduction Act Notice, see the instructions on the back of this form.	Cat. No. 41320P		Form **4070** (Rev. 8-2005)

The employer is responsible for collecting taxes from employee wages for reported tips, and for providing the employer-matched amounts for applicable taxes. If there are not enough employee funds available from which to deduct taxes by the tenth day of the month after the month for which tips are being reported, the company is no longer responsible for collecting any remaining taxes. Where there are not sufficient funds, the company should withhold taxes in the following order:

1. Withhold on regular wages (not tips); then
2. Withhold social security and Medicare taxes on tips; then
3. Withhold income taxes on tips.

If the company is unable to collect some taxes, report the uncollected amounts of social security and Medicare taxes in box 12 of Form W-2 (see the Form W-2 section).

EXAMPLE

Andrew Malone is a waiter at the Boffo Casino's in-house restaurant. He reports $400 in tip income for the preceding month. In addition, Boffo paid him $100 in hourly wages. His wage and tax withholding situation is:

	Wage Income	Tip Income	Total Income
Gross pay	$100.00	$400.00	$500.00
Federal income tax	(20.00)	(80.00)	(100.00)
Social security	(6.20)	(24.80)	(31.00)
Medicare	(1.45)	(5.80)	(7.25)
Total withholdings	$(27.65)	$(110.60)	$(138.25)
Net pay	$72.35	$289.40	$361.75

Boffo's payroll clerk determines that the total withholdings required for Mr. Malone, according to the preceding table, amount to $138.25, and yet the company is only paying him $100 from which to withhold the funds. Thus, the payroll clerk uses the following progression of deductions to reach the $100 maximum withholding:

Priority	Items to Withhold	Withheld	Funds Remaining
1	Withholdings on wages	$(27.65)	$72.35
2	Social security and Medicare on tip income	(30.60)	41.75
3	Income taxes on tip income	41.75	0

The preceding table shows that only $41.75 of income taxes can be withheld from Mr. Malone's tip income, rather than the $80.00 that should be withheld. Mr. Malone is responsible for the $38.25 shortfall.

Types of Payroll Taxes

The government requires employers to pay three types of taxes related to payroll, which are Social Security, Medicare, and unemployment taxes. In the following subsections, we address the nature, amount, and calculation of each tax.

Social Security Tax

The social security tax began with the passage of the Social Security Act in 1935, which established Old Age and Survivor's Insurance. The insurance was to be funded by compulsory deductions from the pay of wage earners. Initially, these deductions were set at 1% of gross wages, and were to be paid by both the employer and the employee, and would continue until retirement age, which was set at 65. By 1948, the amount of these deductions had increased to 3%. Employers have been and continue to be responsible for withholding the social security tax from employee pay.

The tax rate for social security is now governed by the Federal Insurance Contributions Act (FICA). Because of this association, social security taxes are now closely associated with the acronym "FICA".

This tax has increased in size over time, along with the maximum wage cap (also known as the *wage base limit*) to which it applies. The social security tax rate is only applied to a person's wages up to the amount of the wage base cap. Do not apply the tax to any wages earned above the wage cap. For example, on earnings of $150,000 in 2016, the amount of employer tax paid would be $7,347.00, which is calculated as follows:

$$6.2\% \text{ Tax rate} \times \$118,500 \text{ Wage cap} = \$7,347.00$$

The following table shows the recent history of the social security tax for the past few years.

Tax Year	FICA Tax Rate	Wage Cap
2016	6.2%	$118,500
2015	6.2%	118,500
2014	6.2%	117,000

Note that social security is matched by the employee, so the total tax amount paid to the government by the employer is 12.4%.

EXAMPLE

Benjamin Mayhew earned $200,000 in 2016. Based on the $118,500 wage cap in place that year, his employer must deduct $7,347.00 from his gross pay, and match it with another $7,347.00 for a total payment of $14,694.00.

Medicare Tax

Medicare is a health insurance program that is administered by the United States government, and which is primarily available to those 65 years old or older, as well as to those with certain disabilities. It is funded through the Medicare tax, though participants must also pay a portion of all health insurance costs incurred. The program has been in existence since 1965.

Since 1986, the Medicare tax rate that is paid by an employee has been 1.45% (plus matching of the same amount by the employer). There is no cap on the Medicare tax for employed and self-employed people; thus, everyone must pay it, irrespective of the amount of money that they earn.

As of 2014, an additional Medicare tax of 0.9% was imposed, which applies to all wages earned in excess of $250,000 for married filers, and in excess of $200,000 for single and head of household filers.

EXAMPLE

The Armonk Casino employs Mr. Smith, who earns $5,000 of gross pay in the most recent pay period. Armonk withholds $72.50 ($5,000 × .0145) from the pay of Mr. Smith, matches the $72.50 from its own funds, and forwards $145.00 to the government.

Unemployment Taxes

The federal and state governments of the United States provide unemployment compensation to workers who have lost their jobs. This compensation is paid for primarily by employers, who pay both federal and state unemployment taxes.

The FUTA tax rate is 6.0%. Calculate the FUTA tax based on only the first $7,000 paid to each employee in the form of wages during the year (i.e., there is no FUTA tax on wages higher than $7,000 in each calendar year). Then subtract a credit from the FUTA tax for the amount of tax paid into the state unemployment tax fund. The maximum (and most common) amount of this credit is 5.4%, which means that the actual amount of FUTA tax is only 0.6%.

EXAMPLE

The President's Casino employs 100 dealers, all of whom earn more than $100,000 per year. Thus, they all earn more than the $7,000 FUTA wage cap in the first quarter of the year. Within the first quarter, President's has $700,000 of wages eligible for the FUTA tax (calculated as 100 employees × $7,000). Its FUTA tax liability is the 6.0% federal rate minus the 5.4% state rate, multiplied by the $700,000 of eligible wages. President's FUTA tax liability is therefore $4,200 (calculated as $700,000 eligible wages × 0.6%).

FUTA taxes are remitted on a quarterly basis. If the total amount of tax payable is less than $500 in any quarter, the employer can opt to carry the liability forward to the next quarter. The liability can continue to roll forward through additional quarters if the liability remains less than $500.

Each state has its own unemployment insurance program, which evaluates unemployment claims and administers the payment of benefits to individuals. Each of the states has its own rules regarding who is eligible for unemployment benefits, the amounts to be paid, and the duration of those payments, within guidelines set by the federal government.

State governments impose a state-level unemployment tax on employers that can be quite high – even more than the 5.4% credit allowed under FUTA, as noted earlier. A state typically assigns a relatively high default tax rate to a new business, and then subsequently adjusts that rate based on the history of unemployment claims made by employees of the business (known as the *experience rating*). If a business rarely lays off its staff, it will eventually be assigned a lower tax rate, with the reverse being true for a business with an uneven employment record.

States mail unemployment rate notices for the upcoming year to businesses near the end of the current calendar year. Include the tax rate noted on the form in the company's payroll calculations for all of the following year.

Income Tax Withholdings

If an individual is classified as an employee, the employer is responsible for withholding income taxes from that person's gross wages. A key input to the calculation of income tax withholdings is the number of exemptions claimed by an individual on his Form W-4. An example of a completed Form W-4 is provided.

The Form W-4 is completed by each employee, preferably every year, and it contains the number of withholding allowances that they want to claim. Each incremental withholding allowance claimed reduces the amount of federal income tax that the employer must withhold from their pay. When employees complete the Form W-4, they have the option of basing their withholding amount on a fixed dollar amount, a percentage of gross wages, or a percentage of gross wages *and* an additional fixed dollar amount. The amounts specified in the form are the responsibility of the employee, not the company.

> **Tip:** Encourage employees to use the Withholding Calculator located at www.irs.gov/individuals to assist in determining the appropriate number of withholding allowances that they should claim on a Form W-4.

Every employee should complete a Form W-4 when hired, but they are not required by law to do so. If a Form W-4 is not received from an employee, withhold income taxes as though the person were single, with zero withholding allowances (which results in the maximum possible income tax withholding).

Form W-4, Employee's Withholding Allowance Certificate

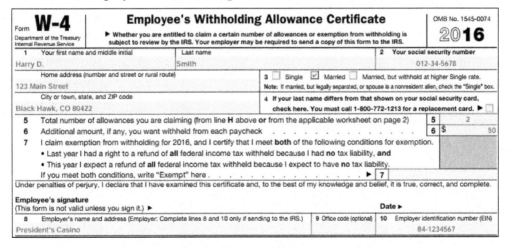

The IRS provides a set of wage bracket tables for income tax withholdings in its Publication 15, Employer's Tax Guide. This publication is available as a PDF download on the www.irs.gov website. The IRS also provides wage bracket tables that show the total amount of the income tax withholding, social security deduction, and Medicare deduction; these tables are published by the IRS in its Publication 15-A, Employer's Supplemental Tax Guide.

The wage bracket tables are designed to be an easy way to derive the correct amount of income tax withholding for people claiming a reasonable number of withholding allowances (up to ten) and at lower wage levels. Each table calculates the proper amount of withholding under a different set of scenarios. Thus, there are separate wage bracket tables that address the following situations:

Payroll Type	Tables within Payroll Type
Daily	Single, Married
Weekly	Single, Married
Biweekly	Single, Married
Monthly	Single, Married

An extract from a combined wage bracket table is shown in the following exhibit, which is taken from the 2015 version of Publication 15-A. The table lists the amount of income tax withholding, social security deduction, and Medicare taxes to be withheld for a married person who is on a biweekly payroll period. The actual table presents information for a much larger range of income, and for more withholding allowances.

IRS Combined Wage Bracket Table for a Married Employee (Biweekly Payroll)

Wages are		The number of withholding allowances claimed is					
At least	But less than	0	1	2	3	4	5
		The amount of income, social security, and Medicare taxes to be withheld is					
1,005	1,025	145.65	130.65	115.65	99.65	84.65	77.65
1,025	1,045	149.18	134.18	119.18	103.18	88.18	79.18
1,045	1,065	153.71	137.71	122.71	106.71	91.71	80.71
1,065	1,085	158.24	141.24	126.24	110.24	95.24	82.24
1,085	1,105	162.77	144.77	129.77	113.77	98.77	83.77
1,105	1,125	167.30	148.30	133.30	117.30	102.30	87.30
1,125	1,145	171.83	151.83	136.83	120.83	105.83	90.83
1,145	1,165	176.36	155.36	140.36	124.36	109.36	94.36
1,165	1,185	180.89	158.89	143.89	127.89	112.89	97.89
1,185	1,205	185.42	162.42	147.42	131.42	116.42	101.42
1,205	1,225	189.95	166.95	150.95	134.95	119.95	104.95

To use the wage bracket method, go to the table that corresponds to the company's payroll period and for the employee's married status (single or married). Within that table, go to the column corresponding to the number of withholding allowances claimed by the employee, and drop down that column until you reach the row corresponding to the wages earned by the employee in the pay period. The amount in that cell represents either the amount of income tax to withhold (if using the Publication 15 table) or the entire amount of income tax, social security, and Medicare to withhold (if using the Publication 15-A table).

EXAMPLE

Albert Montaigne works for the Mountain Casino. Mr. Montaigne is an hourly production employee of the company, which pays its staff on a biweekly basis. Mr. Montaigne earned $1,180 during the most recent biweekly period. He has claimed four withholding allowances on his Form W-4. According to the preceding extract from the IRS combined wage bracket table, the casino should deduct a total of $112.89 from his wages to cover income tax withholdings, as well as social security and Medicare taxes.

> **Tip:** Be certain that the wage bracket tables being used are for the correct year, since the IRS updates the tables every year. If tables from a prior year are used, the wrong amounts are being withheld.

Benefits and Other Deductions

Thus far, we have described a set of mandatory deductions from gross pay related to taxes. In addition, there are a number of other deductions that may be taken from gross pay. The essential information related to these deductions is described in the following bullet points:

- *Benefits deductions.* A company that wants to retain its employees over the long term may offer them a benefits package that could include medical, dental, vision, life, short-term and long-term disability insurance. The amount deducted from employee pay is typically the residual amount owed after the company pays for a portion of the underlying expense.
- *Charitable contributions.* Many employers encourage their employees to make contributions to local or national charities, and may also match these contributions to some extent. Under such an arrangement, an employee signs a pledge card, which authorizes the company to deduct certain contribution amounts from their pay on an ongoing basis. The company then periodically forwards the sum total of all contributions deducted to the targeted charities, along with any matching amount that the company is paying.
- *Garnishments.* Some people resist fulfilling their legal obligations to other parties, or they do not have the financial resources to do so. If the company employs such a person, it is quite possible that the accountant will receive a garnishment order, under which the entity must withhold specified amounts

76

from an employee's pay and forward it to a third party. A garnishment order usually relates to child support, unpaid taxes, or unpaid student loans.

- *Union dues.* If a company has entered into a collective bargaining agreement with a labor union, the terms of the agreement usually stipulate that the company withhold union dues from employee pay and forward it to the union.
- *Deductions for financing repayments.* A business may issue advances or loans to its employees. If so, deductions from future paychecks will be needed to reduce the balances of these outstanding amounts.

Net Pay

Net pay is the amount paid to employees after all of the deductions described in the previous sections are deducted from gross pay. The entire net pay calculation may be included in a remittance advice that is forwarded to employees along with their paychecks. A typical calculation format that may be given to an employee is as follows:

Gross pay (40 hours × $30.00/hour)	$1,200.00
Deductions:	
Social security	74.40
Medicare	17.40
Income tax withholding	225.00
Medical insurance	160.00
Union dues	15.00
Garnishments	100.00
Net pay	$608.20

Remitting Payroll Taxes

An employer has a legal obligation to forward to the government all income taxes that it has withheld from employee pay, as well as social security and Medicare taxes. These remittances must be forwarded to the government in accordance with a specific payment schedule and method that is described in the following subsections. In this section, we review when tax deposits should be made, how to remit funds, and related reporting requirements.

If an employer were to miss a timely remittance, or pay an insufficient amount, the related penalty would be severe. For this reason alone, it is important to have a detailed understanding of tax remittances.

Types of Tax Deposit Schedules

There are two deposit schedules, known as the *monthly deposit schedule* and the *semiweekly deposit schedule* that state when to deposit payroll taxes. You must determine which of these deposit schedules you will follow before the beginning of each calendar year. The selection of a deposit schedule is based entirely on the tax liability reported during a *lookback period*.

The deposit schedule is based on the total taxes (i.e., federal income taxes withheld, social security taxes, and Medicare taxes) reported in line 8 of the Forms 941 in a four-quarter lookback period. The lookback period begins on July 1 and ends on June 30. The decision tree for selecting a deposit period is:

- If the business reported $50,000 or less of taxes during the lookback period, use the monthly deposit schedule.
- If the business reported more than $50,000 of taxes during the lookback period, use the semiweekly deposit schedule.

Note: Do not select a deposit schedule based on how often the company pays employees or makes deposits. It is solely based on the total tax liability reported during the lookback period.

EXAMPLE

The Millionaire Casino had used the monthly deposit schedule in previous years, but its payroll expanded considerably in the past year, which may place it in the semiweekly deposit schedule. Millionaire's accountant calculates the amount of taxes paid during its lookback period to see if the semiweekly deposit schedule now applies. The calculation is:

Lookback Period	Taxes Paid
July 1 – September 30, 2014	$8,250
October 1 – December 31, 2014	14,750
January 1 – March 31, 2015	17,500
April 1 – June 30, 2015	19,000
Total	$59,500

Since the total amount of taxes that Millionaire paid during the lookback period exceeded $50,000, the company must use the semiweekly deposit schedule during the next calendar year.

Tip: A new employer has no lookback period, and so is automatically considered a monthly schedule depositor for its first calendar year of business.

The schedule for depositing state withholding taxes varies by state. Consult with the applicable state government for this deposit schedule. If the business outsources payroll processing, the supplier will handle these deposits on the company's behalf.

Monthly Deposit Schedule

If a business qualifies to use the monthly deposit schedule, deposit employment taxes on payments made during a month by the 15th day of the following month.

EXAMPLE

Joe's Casino is a monthly schedule depositor that pays its staff on the 15th and last business day of each month. Under the monthly deposit schedule, Joe's must deposit the combined tax liabilities for all of its payrolls in a month by the 15th day of the following month. The same deposit schedule would apply if Joe's had instead paid its employees every day, every other week, twice a month, once a month, or on any other payroll schedule.

The total payroll taxes withheld for each of Joe's payrolls in September are noted in the following table, along with the amount of its tax liability that will be due for remittance to the government on October 15:

	Federal Income Tax Withheld	Social Security Tax Withheld	Medicare Tax Withheld
Sept. 15 payroll	$1,500.00	$620.00	$145.00
Sept. 30 payroll	1,250.00	558.00	130.50
Sept. total withheld	$2,750.00	$1,178.00	$275.50
Employer tax matching	--	1,178.00	275.50
Tax deposit due Oct. 15	$2,750.00	$2,356.00	$551.00

Joe's tax liability to be remitted on October 15 is $5,657.00, which is calculated as the total of all withholdings and employer matches for federal income taxes, social security taxes, and Medicare taxes ($2,750.00 + $2,356.00 + $551.00).

Semiweekly Deposit Schedule

If an employer qualifies to use the semiweekly deposit schedule, remit payroll taxes using the following table:

Payment Date	Corresponding Deposit Date
Wednesday, Thursday, or Friday	Following Wednesday
Saturday, Sunday, Monday, Tuesday	Following Friday

If an employer has more than one pay date during a semiweekly period and the pay dates fall in different calendar quarters, make separate deposits for the liabilities associated with each pay date.

EXAMPLE

The Slot Master Casino has a pay date on Wednesday, June 29 (second quarter) and another pay date on Friday, July 1 (third quarter). Slot Master must make a separate deposit for the taxes associated with each pay date, even though both dates fall within the same semiweekly period. The company should pay both deposits on the following Wednesday, July 6.

EXAMPLE

High Pay Slots uses the semiweekly deposit schedule. The company only pays its employees once a month, on the last day of the month. Although High Pay is on a semiweekly deposit schedule, it can only make a deposit once a month, since it only pays its employees once a month.

Note that the semiweekly deposit method does not mean that an employer is required to make two tax deposits per week – it is simply the name of the method. Thus, if a company has one payroll every other week, it would remit taxes only every other week.

The differentiating factor between the monthly and semiweekly deposit schedules is that an employer must remit taxes much more quickly under the semiweekly method. The monthly method uses a simpler and more delayed tax deposit schedule, which is ideal for smaller businesses.

Federal Unemployment Deposit Schedule

The federal unemployment tax is to be deposited on a quarterly basis. The deposit dates are:

Relevant Calendar Quarter	Last Possible Deposit Date
First quarter of the calendar year	April 30
Second quarter of the calendar year	July 31
Third quarter of the calendar year	October 31
Fourth quarter of the calendar year	January 31

Remittance Method

All federal tax deposits must be paid by electronic funds transfer. Use the Electronic Federal Tax Payment System (EFTPS) to make these deposits. EFTPS is a free service that is maintained by the Department of Treasury. The system can either be used directly or through an intermediary, such as the company's payroll supplier (if the business is outsourcing payroll) to deposit the funds on the company's behalf. Go to www.eftps.gov to enroll in EFTPS. If the business is a new employer, it will likely have been pre-enrolled in EFTPS when it applied for an employer identification number (EIN); if so, the company will receive a personal identification number for the EFTPS system as part of the initial EIN package of information.

When remitting taxes to the government, the remittance should include the following types of taxes:

- Withheld income taxes
- Withheld and matching employer social security taxes
- Withheld and matching employer Medicare taxes

When a deposit is made, EFTPS will provide a deposit trace number, which can be used as a receipt or to trace the payment.

The Form 941 Quarterly Federal Tax Return

Following each calendar quarter, any employer that pays wages subject to income tax withholding, or social security and Medicare taxes, must file a Form 941, the Employer's Quarterly Federal Tax Return. The Form 941 must be filed by the last day of the month following the calendar quarter to which it applies. Thus, the filing dates for the Form 941 are:

Quarter Ending	Form 941 Due Date
March 31	April 30
June 30	July 31
September 30	October 31
December 31	January 31

If a Form 941 is not filed in a timely manner (not including filing extensions), the IRS imposes a failure-to-file penalty of 5% of the unpaid tax due with that return, up to a maximum penalty of 25% of the tax due. In addition, for each whole month or part of a month that payment is late, there is an additional failure-to-pay penalty of ½% of the amount of the tax, up to a maximum of 25% of the tax due. If both penalties apply in a month, the failure-to-file penalty is reduced by the amount of the failure-to-pay penalty. The IRS may waive these penalties if a reasonable cause can be presented for failing to file the Form 941 or pay the tax due.

State Tax Remittances

Each state government has its own system for reporting and depositing state-level payroll taxes. The types of taxes can vary from those collected at the federal level, and may include the following:

- State income tax
- Unemployment insurance tax
- Disability insurance tax
- Special district taxes (such as for a transportation district)

The forms used to report this information vary by state. The primary reports that may be required are:

- *Reconciliation statement.* Compares the amount of state taxes remitted to the amount withheld from employee pay.
- *Tax withholdings.* Reports wages paid to employees, and the state taxes withheld from their pay.

Most state governments provide preprinted tax remittance and reporting forms to those employers registered to do business within their boundaries. If an employer outsources its payroll, the supplier is responsible for completing and submitting these forms.

The required remittance dates also vary by state, as do the modes of payment – either check or electronic payments may be required. In some cases, an employer can choose between modes of payment, though it is customary to require electronic payment for all future payments, once an employer has switched to that type of payment.

Each state government publishes an explanatory guide to its tax structure, in which it describes the state's reporting and remittance system. These guides are usually also available online as PDF documents or web pages.

Payments to Employees

The standard method for paying employees for many years was the check, though it has been largely supplanted by direct deposit. A check is usually accompanied by a *remittance advice* (also known as a *check stub*), on which is listed an employee's gross pay, tax deductions and other withholdings, and net pay. A simplified sample remittance advice for a one-week pay period is:

Employee Name: Arturo Johansson							[company name]
Ending Pay Date	Hours Worked	Rate	Gross Pay	Federal Inc. Tax	Social Security	Medicare	Net Pay
5/15/xx	Regular 40 OT 10	$20.00 $30.00	$1,100.00	$197.25	$68.20	$15.95	$818.60

Direct deposit involves the electronic transfer of funds from the company to the bank accounts of its employees, using the Automated Clearing House (ACH) system. ACH is an electronic network for the processing of both debit and credit transactions within the United States and Canada.

The payment process is to calculate pay in the same manner as for check payments, but to then send the payment information to a direct deposit processing service, which initiates electronic payments to the bank accounts of those employees being paid in this manner. The processing service deducts the funds from a company bank account in advance of the direct deposits, so cash flow tends to be somewhat more accelerated than is the case if a company were to issue checks and then wait several days for the amounts on the checks to be withdrawn from its bank account.

Direct deposit is more efficient than payments by check, because it does not require a signature on each payment, there are no checks to be delivered, and employees do not have to waste time depositing them at a bank. Further, employees who are off-site can still rely upon having cash paid into their accounts in a timely manner.

Direct deposit can also be more efficient from the perspective of the remittance advice. A number of payroll suppliers offer an option to simply notify employees by e-mail when their pay has been sent to them, after which employees can access a secure website to view their remittance advice information. This approach is better than sending a paper version of a remittance advice, because employees can also access many years of historical pay information on-line, as well as their W-2 forms.

The implementation of direct deposit can cause some initial difficulties, because each person's bank account information must be correctly set up in the direct deposit module of the company's payroll software (or software provided by the outsourced payroll supplier). This initial setup is remarkably prone to error, and also usually requires a test transaction (the *pre-notification*) that delays implementation by one pay period. Consequently, even if a new employee signs up for direct deposit immediately, the accountant must still print a paycheck for that person's first payroll, after which direct deposit can be used.

Tip: If employees want to be paid by direct deposit, require them to submit a voided check for the checking account into which they want funds to be sent. You can more reliably take the routing and account numbers directly from such a check, rather than risking a transposition error if an employee copies this information onto a form. Also, do not accept a deposit slip instead of a check – the information on the deposit slip may not match the routing and account number information on the check.

A final issue with direct deposit is being able to do so from an in-house payroll processing function. If the payroll software does not provide for direct deposit, it will be necessary to contract with a third party to make the payments on behalf of the company. Direct deposit is much easier to implement if the company is outsourcing payroll, since direct deposit is part of the standard feature set for all payroll suppliers.

The Payroll Register

The primary internal report generated by the payroll system is the payroll register. This document itemizes the calculation of wages, taxes, and deductions for each employee for each payroll. There are multiple uses for the payroll register, including:

- *Investigation.* It is the starting point for the investigation of many issues involving employee pay.
- *Journal entries.* You create journal entries to record a payroll based on the information in the register.

- *Payments*. If you are creating manual check payments, the source document for these payments is the register.
- *Reports*. The information on almost any government or management report related to payroll is drawn from the register.

The format of the payroll register is built into the payroll software, and so will vary somewhat by payroll system. If payroll processing is outsourced, the supplier will issue its own version of the payroll register as part of its basic service package. The following is a typical payroll register format, with overtime and state and local taxes removed in order to compress the presentation:

Sample Payroll Register

Empl. Nbr.	Employee Name	Hours Worked	Rate/ Hour	Gross Wages	Taxes	Other Deductions	Check Nbr.	Net Pay
100	Johnson, Mark	40	18.12	724.80	55.45	28.00	5403	641.35
105	Olds, Gary	27	36.25	978.75	74.87	42.25	5404	861.63
107	Zeff, Morton	40	24.00	960.00	73.44	83.00	5405	803.56
111	Quill, Davis	40	15.00	600.00	45.90	10.10	5406	544.00
116	Pincus, Joseph	35	27.75	971.25	74.30	37.50	5407	859.45

A comprehensive payroll register will include the following fields:
- *Employee number*. This is a unique identification number for each employee. The preceding report is sorted by employee number.
- *Department number*. In larger organizations, it is an excellent idea to assign a department number to each employee, so that departmental wage information can be more easily aggregated and charged to the correct department.
- *Employee name*. This is usually presented in last name, first name format. The payroll register may be sorted by employee last name, rather than by employee number.
- *Salary/wage indicator*. There may be a flag in the report that indicates whether an employee is paid a fixed salary or an hourly wage.
- *Marriage code*. This is a flag in the report, indicating whether a person is classified as married or single. Marriage status impacts the amount of income taxes withheld.
- *Allowances number*. This is the number of allowances that a person has claimed on his or her Form W-4. The number of allowances is used to calculate the amount of income taxes withheld.
- *Total hours worked*. This is the combined total of regular and overtime hours worked, and should tie back to the hours listed in the timekeeping system.
- *Regular hours worked*. This states the total amount of regular hours worked during the payroll period, and is used to calculate gross pay.

- *Overtime hours worked.* This states the total amount of overtime hours worked during the payroll period, and is used to calculate gross pay.
- *Regular hours pay rate.* This rate is multiplied by regular hours worked to arrive at part of the gross pay figure.
- *Overtime hours pay rate.* This rate is multiplied by overtime hours worked to arrive at part of the gross pay figure.
- *Gross pay.* This combines wages paid from regular and overtime hours worked, and is the grand total from which deductions are then made to arrive at net pay.
- *Federal income tax withholding.* This is the federal-level income taxes withheld from employee gross wages.
- *Social security tax.* This is the employee-paid portion of the social security tax. It does not include the employer-matched amount of the tax.
- *Medicare tax.* This is the employee-paid portion of the Medicare tax. It does not include the employer-matched amount of the tax.
- *State income tax withholding.* This is the state income taxes withheld from employee wages.
- *Other deductions.* This can include a broad array of deductions, such as for medical insurance, life insurance, pension plan contributions, and so forth. Identify each type of deduction on the report with a unique code. Thus, deductions for medical insurance could be identified with the MED code, while deductions for life insurance could be identified with the LIFE code.
- *Net pay.* This is the amount of cash paid to each employee after all deductions have been made from gross pay.
- *Check number.* This is the unique identifying number listed on each paycheck issued, and is used by the bank to identify cleared checks (among other uses).
- *Payment type.* This is a code that states whether payment was made with a check, direct deposit, or debit card.

Tip: Do *not* include employee social security numbers in the payroll register, since these reports may end up in the wrong hands, leading to inappropriate dissemination of the social security numbers.

The payroll register should also provide a variety of summary-level information that can be used to record wage and tax information in the general ledger. It should aggregate gross wages, each type of deduction, state-level taxes withheld by individual state, and the total amount of cash paid. If you report at the department level, the payroll register should provide this information not only in total for the entire company, but also at the department level.

If a company were to create a payroll register that contained all of the items in the preceding list, it would be an exceptionally crowded report. However, packing information into the payroll register makes it a great source document when researching payroll issues. Consequently, it is better to create a near-comprehensive payroll register format, rather than one containing the minimum amount of information.

Form W-2

Following the end of every calendar year, and no later than January 31, an employer must issue the multi-part Form W-2, on which it itemizes the wages it paid to each employee during the year, as well as the taxes that it withheld from employee pay. It issues this form to anyone who was paid wages by the company at any time during the year, even if they no longer work for the business. This information forms the basis for the personal income tax returns completed by all employees for the federal government and the state government in which they reside. An example of the Form W-2 is shown below.

Sample Form W-2

The Form W-2 contains a large number of fields, but many of them are not needed to report the compensation and tax information for a typical employee; many of the fields are only required to report unusual compensation arrangements. The payroll system prints these forms automatically after the end of the calendar year. If the organization is outsourcing payroll, the supplier will issue them on the company's behalf. Thus, the Form W-2 is usually not an especially difficult document to produce.

Payroll Journal Entries

The payroll system may be entirely separate from a company's primary system of recording accounting transactions. This is especially true if it has outsourced the payroll function entirely. Thus, the accountant will need a process for transferring the information accumulated in the payroll system to the accounting system. The chief tool for doing so is the journal entry, which is used to transfer a variety of types of expense-related information at a summary level into the accounting system. This section describes where payroll information is stored in an accounting system, and the journal entries used to record payroll information in that system.

> **Note:** The accounting system does not contain information about employee-specific wage and benefit information. The payroll system must be accessed to obtain this information.

Types of Payroll Journal Entries

There are several types of journal entries that involve the recordation of compensation. The primary entry is for the initial recordation of a payroll. This entry records the gross wages earned by employees, as well as all withholdings from their pay, and any additional taxes owed by the company. There may also be an accrued wages entry that is recorded at the end of each accounting period, and which is intended to record the amount of wages owed to employees but not yet paid. These types of compensation are based on different source documents and require separate calculations and journal entries. There are also a number of other payroll-related journal entries that a payroll staff must deal with on a regular basis. They include:

- Manual paychecks
- Employee advances
- Accrued vacation pay
- Tax deposits

All of these journal entries are described in the following sub-sections.

Primary Payroll Journal Entry

The primary journal entry for payroll is the summary-level entry that is compiled from the payroll register. This entry usually includes debits for the direct labor expense, wages, and the company's portion of payroll taxes. There will also be credits to a number of other accounts, each one detailing the liability for payroll taxes that have not been paid, as well as for the amount of cash already paid to employees for their net pay. The basic entry (assuming no further breakdown of debits by individual department) is:

Payroll Accounting

	Debit	Credit
Wages expense	xxx	
Payroll taxes expense	xxx	
Cash		xxx
Federal withholding taxes payable		xxx
Social security taxes payable		xxx
Medicare taxes payable		xxx
Federal unemployment taxes payable		xxx
State unemployment taxes payable		xxx
Garnishments payable		xxx

> **Note:** The reason for the payroll taxes expense line item in this journal entry is that the company incurs the cost of matching the social security and Medicare amounts paid by employees, and directly incurs the cost of unemployment insurance. The employee-paid portions of the social security and Medicare taxes are not recorded as expenses; instead, they are liabilities for which the company has an obligation to remit cash to the taxing government entity.

A key point with this journal entry is that the wages expense contains employee gross pay, while the amount actually paid to employees through the cash account is their net pay. The difference between the two figures (which can be substantial) is the amount of deductions from their pay, such as payroll taxes and withholdings to pay for benefits.

There may be a number of additional employee deductions to include in this journal entry. For example, there may be deductions for 401(k) pension plans, health insurance, life insurance, vision insurance, and for the repayment of advances.

When the company later pays the withheld taxes and company portion of payroll taxes, use the following entry to reduce the balance in the cash account, and eliminate the balances in the liability accounts:

	Debit	Credit
Federal withholding taxes payable	xxx	
Social security taxes payable	xxx	
Medicare taxes payable	xxx	
Federal unemployment taxes payable	xxx	
State withholding taxes payable	xxx	
State unemployment taxes payable	xxx	
Garnishments payable	xxx	
Cash		xxx

Thus, when a company initially deducts taxes and other items from an employee's pay, the company incurs a liability to pay the taxes to a third party. This liability only disappears from the company's accounting records when it pays the related funds to the entity to which they are owed.

Accrued Wages

It is quite common to have some amount of unpaid wages at the end of an accounting period, so accrue this expense (if it is material). The accrual entry, as shown next, is simpler than the comprehensive payroll entry already shown, because all payroll taxes are typically clumped into a single expense account and offsetting liability account. After recording this entry, reverse it at the beginning of the following accounting period, and then record the actual payroll expense whenever it occurs.

	Debit	Credit
Wages expense	xxx	
Accrued salaries and wages		xxx
Accrued payroll taxes		xxx

The information for the wage accrual entry is most easily derived from a spreadsheet that itemizes all employees to whom the calculation applies, the amount of unpaid time, and the standard pay rate for each person. It is not necessary to also calculate the cost of overtime hours earned during an accrual period if the amount of such hours is relatively small. A sample spreadsheet for calculating accrued wages is:

Hourly Employees	Unpaid Days	Hourly Rate	Pay Accrual
Anthem, Jill	4	$20.00	$640
Bingley, Adam	4	18.25	584
Chesterton, Elvis	4	17.50	560
Davis, Ethel	4	23.00	736
Ellings, Humphrey	4	21.50	688
Fogarty, Miriam	4	16.00	512
		Total	$3,720

Manual Paycheck Entry

It is all too common to create a manual paycheck, either because an employee was short-paid in a prior payroll, or because the company is laying off or firing an employee, and so is obligated to pay that person before the next regularly scheduled payroll. This check may be paid through the corporate accounts payable bank account, rather than its payroll account, so it may be necessary to make this entry through the accounts payable system.

EXAMPLE

The High Noon Casino lays off Mr. Jones. High Noon owes Mr. Jones $5,000 of wages at the time of the layoff. The accountant calculates that High Noon must withhold $382.50 from Mr. Jones' pay to cover the employee-paid portions of social security and Medicare taxes. Mr. Jones has claimed a large enough number of withholding allowances that there is no income tax withholding. Thus, the company pays Mr. Jones $4,617.50. The journal entry it uses is:

	Debit	Credit
Wage expense	5,000	
Social security taxes payable		310.00
Medicare taxes payable		72.50
Cash		4,617.50

At the next regularly-scheduled payroll, the accountant records this payment as a notation in the payroll system, so that it will properly compile the correct amount of wages for Mr. Jones for his year-end Form W-2. In addition, the payroll system calculates that High Noon must pay a matching amount of social security and Medicare taxes (though no unemployment taxes, since Mr. Jones already exceeded his wage cap for these taxes). Accordingly, an additional liability of $382.50 is recorded in the payroll journal entry for that payroll. High Noon pays these matching amounts as part of its normal tax remittances associated with the payroll.

Employee Advances

When an employee asks for an advance, this is recorded as a current asset in the company's balance sheet. There may not be a separate account in which to store advances, especially if employee advances are infrequent; possible asset accounts that can be used are:
- Employee advances (for high-volume situations)
- Other assets (probably sufficient for smaller companies that record few assets other than trade receivables, inventory, and fixed assets)
- Other receivables (useful if the accountant is tracking a number of different types of assets, and wants to segregate receivables in one account)

EXAMPLE

The High Noon Casino issues a $1,000 advance to employee Wes Smith. High Noon issues advances regularly, and so uses a separate account in which to record advances. It records the transaction as:

	Debit	Credit
Other assets	1,000	
Cash		1,000

One week later, Mr. Smith pays back half the amount of the advance, which is recorded with this entry:

	Debit	Credit
Cash	500	
Other assets		500

No matter what method is later used to repay the company – a check from the employee, or payroll deductions – the entry will be a credit to whichever asset account was used, until such time as the balance in the account has been paid off.

Employee advances require vigilance by the accountant, because employees who have limited financial resources will tend to use the company as their personal banks, and so will be reluctant to pay back advances unless pressed repeatedly. Thus, it is essential to continually monitor the remaining amount of advances outstanding for every employee.

Accrued Vacation Pay

Accrued vacation pay is the amount of vacation time that an employee has earned as per a company's employee benefit manual, but which he has not yet used. The calculation of accrued vacation pay for each employee is:

1. Calculate the amount of vacation time earned through the beginning of the accounting period. This should be a roll-forward balance from the preceding period.
2. Add the number of hours earned in the current accounting period.
3. Subtract the number of vacation hours used in the current period.
4. Multiply the ending number of accrued vacation hours by the employee's hourly wage to arrive at the correct accrual that should be on the company's books.
5. If the amount already accrued for the employee from the preceding period is lower than the correct accrual, record the difference as an addition to the accrued liability. If the amount already accrued from the preceding period is higher than the correct accrual, record the difference as a reduction of the accrued liability.

A sample spreadsheet follows that uses the preceding steps, and which can be used to compile accrued vacation pay:

Name	Vacation Roll-Forward Balance	+ New Hours Earned	- Hours Used	= Net Balance	× Hourly Pay	= Accrued Vacation $
Hilton, David	24.0	10	34.0	0.0	$25.00	$0.00
Idle, John	13.5	10	0.0	23.5	17.50	411.25
Jakes, Jill	120.0	10	80.0	50.0	23.50	1,175.00
Kilo, Steve	114.5	10	14.0	110.5	40.00	4,420.00
Linder, Alice	12.0	10	0.0	22.0	15.75	346.50
Mills, Jeffery	83.5	10	65.00	28.5	19.75	562.88
					Total	$6,915.63

It is not necessary to reverse the vacation pay accrual in each period if you choose to instead record just incremental changes in the accrual from month to month.

EXAMPLE

There is already an existing accrued balance of 40 hours of unused vacation time for Wes Smith on the books of the High Noon Casino. In the most recent month that has just ended, Mr. Smith accrued an additional five hours of vacation time (since he is entitled to 60 hours of accrued vacation time per year, and 60 ÷ 12 = five hours per month). He also used three hours of vacation time during the month. This means that, as of the end of the month, High Noon should have accrued a total of 42 hours of vacation time for him (calculated as 40 hours existing balance + 5 hours additional accrual − 3 hours used).

Mr. Smith is paid $30 per hour, so his total vacation accrual should be $1,260 (42 hours × $30/hour), so High Noon accrues an additional $60 of vacation liability.

What if an employee receives a pay raise? Then it will be necessary to increase the amount of his entire vacation accrual by the incremental amount of the pay raise. This is because, if the employee were to leave the company and be paid all of his unused vacation pay, he would be paid at his most recent rate of pay.

Tax Deposits

When an employer withholds taxes from employee pay, it must deposit these funds with the government at stated intervals. The journal entry for doing so is a debit to the tax liability account being paid and a credit to the cash account, which reduces the cash balance. For example, if a company were to pay a state government for unemployment taxes, the entry would be:

	Debit	Credit
State unemployment taxes payable	xxx	
Cash		xxx

Summary

The payroll function is one of the most crucial accounting operations, since employees are depending on the accountant to correctly determine gross pay, deductions, and net pay – every time. If a casino has a continuing problem with payments to employees, this can trigger significant employee dissatisfaction. There are several ways to mitigate payroll errors, which include the following:

- Upgrade the timekeeping system from timecards to an electronic time clock, so that employee hours worked are automatically recorded in the payroll software.
- Outsource payroll processing to a third party. By doing so, a specialist is now being involved in payroll calculations, taxes remittances, and payments to employees. This does not completely eliminate errors, since the accountant must still input information into the third party's system – but errors should decline.
- Use formal procedures as part of every payroll processing activity. Doing so reduces the risk that steps will be missed or completed incorrectly. This is especially important when the accountant is new to payroll processing.

Chapter 5
Receivables and Payables Accounting

Introduction

One of the most fundamental accounting tasks is the accounting for and collection of markers. If customer statements and payment receipts are not correctly prepared and recorded, there will be incorrect receivable records, as well as trouble collecting from customers. In this chapter, we describe how unpaid markers are accounted for, as well as the use of credit memos, the allowance for doubtful accounts, and similar topics.

The offset of accounts receivable is accounts payable, where a casino identifies payment obligations to suppliers and prepares payments to them. In this chapter, we address the accounting for accounts payable, as well as reporting for 1099 vendors.

Related Podcast Episodes: Episodes 81, 82, and 138 discuss how to improve the accounts payable function. They are available at: **accountingtools.com/podcasts** or **iTunes**

Accounting for Accounts Receivable

Casinos prefer to have their customers settle all outstanding marker balances when they leave the casino. Nonetheless, there are instances in which a marker balance remains outstanding after an individual leaves. If so, the outstanding amount is loaded in the accounting software as an account receivable. To do so, the accountant loads in the customer's name and address, the unique marker number, and the amount outstanding, as well as the date. Once finished, the software automatically creates a journal entry for the transaction.

When a customer pays for a marker, the usual process is to cut a check which states the marker number being paid. Upon receipt of this check, the accountant enters the payment into the cash receipts module of the accounting software, using the customer name and marker number to locate the applicable marker in the system. Once the entry is recorded, the software automatically creates a journal entry to clear out the accounts receivable balance for the marker and increase the cash balance. The entry is:

	Debit	Credit
Cash (asset)	xxx	
Accounts receivable (asset)		xxx

94

A casino may accept a partial write down on an outstanding marker amount in exchange for payment of the remaining amount. This step may be taken in order to retain the business of a customer in the future.

EXAMPLE

Pirates Casino has a marker outstanding with Mr. Jones for $10,000. Pirates offers Mr. Jones a $2,000 discount if he pays the remaining balance. He does so, and sends in a payment of $8,000. The resulting entry is:

	Debit	Credit
Cash (asset)	8,000	
Allowance for doubtful accounts (contra asset)	2,000	
Accounts receivable (asset)		10,000

There may be cases in which a customer refuses to pay all or a portion of a marker. If so, the accountant records a credit in the accounting software that offsets the applicable marker. This transaction is usually documented via a credit memo, which explains the reason for the credit, the amount, and the number of the marker that is to be offset by the credit. A sample credit memo approval form is shown below.

Sample Credit Memo Approval Form

Credit Memo Approval Form

| Customer Name | | Credit Memo ▢ |
| Customer Number | | Internal Credit Memo ▢ |

| Credit Amount Requested | Reason for Request |

| Marker to Offset (if any) |

| Supervisor Approval Block |

There are two varieties of credit memo, each one serving a different purpose. A customer may be notified of an external credit memo, stating that a specific marker balance has been written off. However, there may be a situation in which the accounting staff is still attempting to collect a balance, but does not expect to do so, and so wants to use a credit memo to write off the marker balance. An internal credit memo is used in the latter situation, which is not mailed to the customer. Otherwise, the customer might receive the credit memo and use it as evidence that no payment is required.

Collections

The collections function operates in a manner similar to the function in any other industry, with a few variations. One alteration is that some customers do not want the casino to send them a statement of amounts owed, perhaps because they do not want the amount of their losses accidentally discovered by anyone else in their household. If so, these customers specify that they will pay the outstanding amount by a specific date, without any notification. Otherwise, a statement is sent shortly after a customer leaves the casino.

The information for outstanding receivables appears in a receivables aging report, which clusters invoices by date range. This report is the primary tool used to determine which invoices are overdue for payment. Given its use as a collection tool, the report may be configured to also contain contact information for each customer. The report is also used by management, to determine the effectiveness of credit and collection activities.

A typical aging report lists invoices in 30-day "buckets," where the columns contain the following information:

- The left-most column contains all invoices that are 30 days old or less
- The next column contains invoices that are 31-60 days old
- The next column contains invoices that are 61-90 days old
- The final column contains all older invoices

The use of these time buckets to categorize receivables is important, since receivables rapidly lose their value after three months, and are essentially uncollectible after six months.

The report is sorted by customer name, with all invoices for each customer itemized directly below the customer name, usually sorted by either invoice number or invoice date. A sample report follows, though without the individual invoice detail that is usually found in such a report:

Sample Receivables Aging Report

Customer Name	Total Receivable	0-30 Days	31-60 Days	61-90 Days	90+ Days
Albertson, David	$15,000	$10,000	$5,000		
Bufford, Glen	29,000		20,000	$9,000	
Chesterton, Lord	83,000	47,000	21,000	12,000	$3,000
Dingle, David	8,000				8,000
Totals	$135,000	$57,000	$46,000	$21,000	$11,000

A customer may pay a marker with a post-dated check, giving the casino instructions to not cash the check until the date stated on the check. As a customer courtesy, the accounting staff may contact the bank on which the check is drawn as of the check date, to verify that there are sufficient funds in the customer's account to ensure that the check will clear. Doing so keeps a customer from receiving an embarrassing not sufficient funds notice from their bank.

If the balance is unpaid by the specified date, then the collections staff calls to inquire about payment. Additional actions may be required, including setting up payment terms or threatening to eliminate comps for future trips. Casinos are reluctant to settle for prolonged payment terms, since customers are highly unlikely to return to the casino until all payments have been made.

If all collection efforts fail, the collections manager may choose to turn over an account to an outside collection agency. Outside collection agencies are expensive and can be excessively aggressive in their collection activities, so this is considered to be one of the last activities attempted. Also, it is customary for the accounting department to write off a marker once it is forwarded to a collection agency, on the grounds that it is now probable that payment will not be received.

An alternative is to settle for a reduced amount in exchange for immediate payment of the remainder. Once this payment is received, the remaining amount outstanding is written off. This means that the associated marker is cancelled.

The collections team works closely with the credit granting group, so that customer credit levels can be adjusted (or eliminated) to reflect the proven payment capabilities of each customer.

The collections process in a casino requires more diplomacy with customers than is necessarily the case in other industries, since customers represent long-term revenue streams for a casino. If a customer has a long track record of paying his debts, then a temporary problem with his cash flows is more likely to be handled in an understanding manner, waiting for the person to clear up the problem and resume payments. Conversely, a casino might not want to acquire a reputation for writing off its receivables too quickly, and so could aggressively pursue a few of its customers for unpaid amounts – though preferably only those customers with which it does not intend to do business in the future.

Accounting for Bad Debts

It is quite likely that some markers will never be paid. If so, the accountant must write off these markers as bad debts. There are two ways to do so, which are covered in this section under the headings of the direct write-off method and the allowance for doubtful accounts.

Direct Write-Off Method

The direct write-off method is the practice of charging bad debts to expense in the period when individual markers have been clearly identified as bad debts. The specific activity needed to write off an account receivable under this method is to create a credit memo for the customer in question, which exactly offsets the amount of the bad debt. Creating the credit memo will require a debit to a bad debt expense account and a credit to the accounts receivable account.

The direct write off method delays the recognition of expenses related to a revenue-generating transaction, and so is considered an excessively aggressive accounting method, making a casino appear more profitable in the short term than it really is. For example, a casino may recognize $20,000 in revenue in one month, then wait three or four months to collect the related marker balance, before finally charging some portions of it to the bad debt expense. This creates a lengthy delay between revenue recognition and the recognition of expenses that are directly related to that revenue. Thus, the profit in the initial month is overstated, while profit is understated in the month when the bad debts are finally charged to expense.

The direct write off method can be considered a reasonable accounting method if the amount that is written off is an immaterial amount, since doing so has a minimal impact on a casino's reported financial results.

Allowance for Doubtful Accounts

The allowance for doubtful accounts is a reduction of the total amount of accounts receivable appearing on a casino's balance sheet. This allowance represents management's best estimate of the amount of accounts receivable that will not be paid in the future by customers. There are several ways to derive the amount of this allowance, including the following:

- *Historical percentage*. If a certain percentage of accounts receivable became bad debts in the past, then use the same percentage to estimate future bad debts. This method works best for large numbers of small account balances.
- *Pareto analysis*. Individually review the largest accounts receivable that make up 80% of the total receivable balance, and estimate which specific customers are most likely to default. Then use the preceding historical percentage method for the remaining smaller accounts. This method works best if there are a small number of large account balances.

A common way to derive the amount of the allowance is to assume that an increasing percentage of bad debt applies to each date range listed in the receivables aging report, on the theory that more overdue markers are more likely to not be collected. For example, the following receivables aging report includes an estimated percentage of uncollectible receivables at the bottom of each date range, which is then used to arrive at a total estimated amount of bad debts that will occur.

Sample Estimated Bad Debt Calculation

Customer Name	Total Receivable	0-30 Days	31-60 Days	61-90 Days	90+ Days
Albertson, David	$15,000	$10,000	$5,000		
Bufford, Glen	29,000		20,000	$9,000	
Chesterton, Lord	83,000	47,000	21,000	12,000	$3,000
Dingle, David	8,000				8,000
Totals	$135,000	$57,000	$46,000	$21,000	$11,000
Estimated uncollectible percentage		2%	6%	15%	30%
Total estimated bad debts	$10,350	$1,140	$2,760	$3,150	$3,300

If a casino is using the accrual basis of accounting, it should record an allowance for doubtful accounts, since this approach provides an estimate of future bad debts that improves the accuracy of the financial statements. Also, by recording the allowance at the same time it records a sale, it is properly matching the projected bad debt expense against the related revenue in the same period, which provides a more accurate view of the true profitability of revenues.

For example, a company records $10,000 of revenue from several dozen customers, and projects (based on historical experience) that it will incur 1% of this amount as bad debts, though it does not know exactly which customers will default. It records the 1% of projected bad debts as a $100 debit to the bad debt expense account and a $100 credit to the allowance for doubtful accounts, as follows:

	Debit	Credit
Bad debt expense	100	
Allowance for doubtful accounts		100

The bad debt expense is charged to expense right away, and the allowance for doubtful accounts becomes a reserve account that offsets the account receivable of $10,000 (for a net receivable outstanding of $9,900).

Later, a customer defaults on a marker totaling $80. Accordingly, the accountant uses a credit memo to credit the accounts receivable account by $80, which reduces the amount of outstanding accounts receivable, and debits the allowance for doubtful accounts by $80, as follows:

	Debit	Credit
Allowance for doubtful accounts	80	
Accounts receivable		80

This entry reduces the balance in the allowance account to $20. The entry does not impact earnings in the current period.

At a later date, the customer that previously defaulted makes a $25 payment on the receivable that had been written off. This requires two transactions to record. First, a debit memo is created to reverse the prior write-off of the account receivable, but only in the amount of $25. The entry is:

	Debit	Credit
Accounts receivable	25	
Allowance for doubtful accounts		25

This means there is now a receivable in the accounting database that can be charged with the $25 cash receipt, which is accomplished with the following entry:

	Debit	Credit
Cash	25	
Accounts receivable		25

Given the difficulty of reversing a written-off receivable, many accountants like to leave receivables outstanding for a relatively long period of time before writing them off.

Accounting for Accounts Payable

Accounts payable refers to the collective obligation to pay suppliers for goods and services that were acquired on credit. The day-to-day accounting for accounts payable is relatively simple. Whenever a casino receives an invoice from a supplier, the accountant enters the vendor number of the supplier into the accounting software, which automatically assigns a default general ledger account number from the vendor master file to the invoice. The vendor master file contains essential information about each supplier, including a default account number to which it is assumed that most invoices from that supplier will be charged.

EXAMPLE

The Milagro Casino receives an invoice from Maid Marian, which provides the casino's hotel with cleaning services. In the vendor master file, the accountant has already assigned general ledger account number 852, Cleaning Expenses, to Maid Marian. Thus, when the accountant enters the invoice into the accounts payable module of the accounting software, the system automatically assigns the invoice to account 852.

If the invoice is for goods or services other than the predetermined general ledger account number, the accountant can manually enter a different account number, which is only good for that specific invoice – it does not become the new default account for that supplier. In short, the pre-assignment of account numbers to suppliers greatly simplifies the accounting for payables.

Tip: At the end of each accounting period, print a report that shows the amount of expense charged to each account in each of the past 12 months. Compare the expense balance in the most current period to prior periods; if there is a significant difference, it may be caused by the incorrect assignment of a supplier invoice to an account. If so, investigate the account and see if a different default account should be assigned to the supplier whose invoice caused the discrepancy.

The accounting software should automatically create a credit to the accounts payable account whenever the accountant records a supplier invoice. Thus, a typical entry might be:

	Debit	Credit
Supplies expense (expense)	xxx	
Accounts payable (liability)		xxx

Later, when the company pays suppliers, the accounting system eliminates the accounts payable balance with the following entry:

	Debit	Credit
Accounts payable (liability)	xxx	
Cash (asset)		xxx

It is possible that small debit or credit residual balances may appear in the accounts payable account. These balances may be caused by any number of issues, such as credit memos issued by suppliers which the casino does not plan to use, or amounts that the company had valid cause not to pay. Occasionally run the aged accounts payable report to spot these items. Do not use journal entries to clear them out, since this will not be recognized by the report writing software that generates the aged accounts payable report. Instead, always create debit or credit memo transactions that are recognized by the report writer; this will flush the residual balances from the aged accounts payable report.

There is usually an option in the accounting software that automatically generates the necessary debit memo or credit memo. As an example, a casino may have been granted a credit memo by a supplier for $100, to be used to reduce the amount of an outstanding account payable. The accountant enters the credit memo screen in the accounting software, enters the name of the supplier and the credit memo amount, and selects the expense account that will be offset. The journal entry that the software automatically generates could be as follows:

	Debit	Credit
Accounts payable	100	
Supplies expense		100

If a supplier offers a discount in exchange for the early payment of an invoice, the casino is not paying the full amount of the invoice. Instead, that portion of the invoice related to the discount is charged to a separate account. If an accounting software package is used, the system automatically allocates the appropriate amount to this separate account. For example, an entry to take a 2% early payment discount on a supplier invoice might be:

	Debit	Credit
Accounts payable	100	
Cash		98
Discounts taken		2

This entry flushes out the full amount of the original account payable, so that no residual balance remains in the accounting records to be paid.

At month-end, it may be necessary to accrue for expenses when goods or services have been received by the casino, but for which no supplier invoice has yet been received. To do so, examine the receiving log just after month-end to see which receipts do not have an associated invoice. Also, consider reviewing the expense accruals for the preceding month; a supplier that issues invoices late will probably do so on a repetitive basis, so the last set of expense accruals typically provides clues to what should be included in the next set of accruals.

When a month-end expense accrual is created, it is done with a reversing journal entry, so that the accounting system automatically reverses the expense at the beginning of the following month. Otherwise, the accountant will be at risk of forgetting that an expense was accrued, and may leave it on the books for a number of months. Also, charge the accrued expense to a liability account separate from the accounts payable account, so that all accruals are separately tracked. A common liability account for this is "accrued accounts payable." Thus, a typical accrued expense entry might be:

	Debit	Credit
Rent expense (expense)	xxx	
Accrued accounts payable (liability)		xxx

If a period-end accrual is made for income taxes, the tax could be recorded within the accrued accounts payable account. Alternatively, it could be recorded separately, especially if the amount is so large that management wants to report it separately in the balance sheet. An example of such an entry is:

	Debit	Credit
Income tax expense (expense)	xxx	
Accrued income taxes (liability)		xxx

The 1099 Vendor

A 1099 vendor is a designation, or flag, listed in each of the records in the vendor master file that is part of an accounting software package. If a supplier is designated as a 1099 vendor, the system will print a Form 1099 for the supplier as part of the 1099 batch processing that follows the end of the calendar year. The company then sends the resulting 1099 form to the supplier, which the supplier should use for tax filing purposes. A sample Form 1099 follows.

Sample Form 1099

The software should not print a Form 1099 for any supplier for which the company has issued cumulative payments for the full calendar year of less than $600.

The accountant sends a copy of this report to the Internal Revenue Service (IRS). The intent of the 1099 vendor designation is to ensure that suppliers report the correct amount of income to the IRS for income tax reporting purposes.

The 1099 vendor designation should be applied to any supplier that has the following characteristics (this is a partial list):

- Professional services fees
- Commissions paid to non-employees
- Fees paid to independent contractors
- Taxable fringe benefits for non-employees
- Director's fees
- Fish purchased for cash
- Golden parachute payments

Generally, this designation is for a supplier entity that is not a corporation.

The best practice for designating a 1099 vendor is to have all suppliers fill out and submit a Form W-9, Request for Taxpayer Identification Number and Certification, before paying them. One can then infer from the Form W-9 what the proper designation should be. A sample Form W-9 follows.

Sample Form W-9

Form **W-9** (Rev. December 2014) Department of the Treasury Internal Revenue Service	**Request for Taxpayer** **Identification Number and Certification**	**Give Form to the requester. Do not send to the IRS.**

1 Name (as shown on your income tax return). Name is required on this line; do not leave this line blank.

Wilson Brothers Card and Dice Supplies

2 Business name/disregarded entity name, if different from above

3 Check appropriate box for federal tax classification; check only **one** of the following seven boxes:

☐ Individual/sole proprietor or single-member LLC   ☑ C Corporation   ☐ S Corporation   ☐ Partnership   ☐ Trust/estate

☐ Limited liability company. Enter the tax classification (C=C corporation, S=S corporation, P=partnership) ▶ _____

Note. For a single-member LLC that is disregarded, do not check LLC; check the appropriate box in the line above for the tax classification of the single-member owner.

☐ Other (see instructions) ▶

4 Exemptions (codes apply only to certain entities, not individuals; see instructions on page 3):

Exempt payee code (if any) _____

Exemption from FATCA reporting code (if any) _____

(Applies to accounts maintained outside the U.S.)

5 Address (number, street, and apt. or suite no.)

567 Wilfred Avenue

Requester's name and address (optional)

6 City, state, and ZIP code

Denver, CO 80202

7 List account number(s) here (optional)

Print or type — See Specific Instructions on page 2.

Part I   Taxpayer Identification Number (TIN)

Enter your TIN in the appropriate box. The TIN provided must match the name given on line 1 to avoid backup withholding. For individuals, this is generally your social security number (SSN). However, for a resident alien, sole proprietor, or disregarded entity, see the Part I instructions on page 3. For other entities, it is your employer identification number (EIN). If you do not have a number, see *How to get a TIN* on page 3.

Note. If the account is in more than one name, see the instructions for line 1 and the chart on page 4 for guidelines on whose number to enter.

Social security number

☐ ☐ ☐ – ☐ ☐ – ☐ ☐ ☐ ☐

or

Employer identification number

8 4 – 9 8 7 6 5 4 3

Part II   Certification

Under penalties of perjury, I certify that:

1. The number shown on this form is my correct taxpayer identification number (or I am waiting for a number to be issued to me); and

2. I am not subject to backup withholding because: (a) I am exempt from backup withholding, or (b) I have not been notified by the Internal Revenue Service (IRS) that I am subject to backup withholding as a result of a failure to report all interest or dividends, or (c) the IRS has notified me that I am no longer subject to backup withholding; and

3. I am a U.S. citizen or other U.S. person (defined below); and

4. The FATCA code(s) entered on this form (if any) indicating that I am exempt from FATCA reporting is correct.

Certification instructions. You must cross out item 2 above if you have been notified by the IRS that you are currently subject to backup withholding because you have failed to report all interest and dividends on your tax return. For real estate transactions, item 2 does not apply. For mortgage interest paid, acquisition or abandonment of secured property, cancellation of debt, contributions to an individual retirement arrangement (IRA), and generally, payments other than interest and dividends, you are not required to sign the certification, but you must provide your correct TIN. See the instructions on page 3.

Sign Here   Signature of U.S. person ▶   Date ▶

It is also a good practice to have the Form W-9 updated on an annual basis, so that the casino continues to have the most recent mailing address on file for each supplier. Doing so always warns of any organizational changes in a supplier; this is useful for updating the 1099 flag in the accounting software.

Summary

There are several key issues to consider when recording receivable and payable transactions. First, outstanding marker balances should be recorded as receivables as soon as a customer leaves the casino. If there is any delay, the collections staff will not know that they must begin collection activities.

A second issue is that there should be an approval process in place for ensuring that supplier invoices have been properly authorized. This can be ignored for small invoices, but may involve the use of purchase orders for larger obligations, as well as matching receiving documentation to the supplier invoice.

A final issue is that the accountant should rarely use a journal entry when recording receivable or payable transactions. Instead, use the modules already set up in the accounting software for these transactions; these modules will automatically create entries, which will result in the correct formulation of accounts receivable and payable aging reports. Directly created journal entries will not populate these reports, which results in account balances that do not match the associated detailed reports.

Chapter 6
Fixed Asset Accounting

Introduction

Casinos can require massive investments in facilities, especially when there are many ancillary services, such as hotels, conference facilities, parking garages, and restaurants. If so, the accountant must create classifications for them, decide which expenditures to record as assets, and depreciate them over time. This chapter delves into the types of asset classifications, the capitalization limit, the concept of base units, different types of depreciation, and other issues relating to the proper accounting for fixed assets. Of particular interest is asset impairment, since changes in gaming legislation can have a major impact on the viability of assets.

> **Related Podcast Episode:** Episode 139 of the Accounting Best Practices Podcast discusses a lean system for fixed assets accounting. It is available at: **accounting-tools.com/podcasts** or **iTunes**

What are Fixed Assets?

The vast majority of the expenditures that a casino makes are for consumables, such as staff compensation or meals in the adjacent restaurant. The effect of these items passes through the organization quickly – they are used or sold and converted to cash, and they are recorded as expenses immediately or with a slight delay. Thus, the benefits they generate are short-lived.

Fixed assets are entirely different. These are items that generate economic benefits over a long period of time. Because of the long period of usefulness of a fixed asset, it is not justifiable to charge its entire cost to expense when incurred. Instead, the *matching principle* comes into play. Under the matching principle, an entity should recognize both the benefits and expenses associated with a transaction (or, in this case, an asset) at the same time. To do so, we convert an expenditure into an asset, and use depreciation to gradually charge it to expense.

By designating an expenditure as a fixed asset, we are shifting the expenditure away from the income statement, where expenditures normally go, and instead place it in the balance sheet. As we gradually reduce its recorded cost through depreciation, the expenditure flows from the balance sheet to the income statement. Thus, the main difference between a normal expenditure and a fixed asset is that the fixed asset is charged to expense over a longer period of time.

The process of identifying fixed assets, recording them as assets, and depreciating them is time-consuming, so it is customary to build some limitations into the process that will route most expenditures directly to expense. One such limitation is to charge an expenditure to expense immediately unless it has a useful life of at least one year. Another limitation is to only recognize an expenditure as a fixed asset if it exceeds a certain dollar amount, known as the *capitalization limit*. These limits keep the vast majority of expenditures from being classified as fixed assets, which reduces the work of the accountant.

EXAMPLE

Hilltop Casino incurs expenditures for three items, and the accountant must decide whether it should classify them as fixed assets. Hilltop's capitalization limit is $2,500. The expenditures are:

- It buys a used roulette wheel for $3,000. The accountant expects that the wheel only has six months of useful life left, after which it should be scrapped. Since the useful life is so short, the accountant elects to charge the expenditure to expense immediately.
- It buys a laptop computer for $1,500, which has a useful life of three years. This expenditure is less than the capitalization limit, so it is charged to expense.
- It constructs a new gaming pit area for $200,000, which has a useful life of 10 years. Since this expenditure has a useful life of longer than one year and a cost greater than the capitalization limit, the accountant records it as a fixed asset, and will depreciate it over its 10-year useful life.

An alternative treatment of the $3,000 roulette wheel in the preceding example would be to record it under the Other Assets account in the balance sheet, and charge the cost to expense over six months. This is a reasonable alternative for expenditures that have useful lives of greater than one accounting period, but less than one year. It is a less time-consuming alternative for the accountant, who does not have to create a fixed asset record or engage in any depreciation calculations.

Fixed Asset Classifications

If an expenditure qualifies as a fixed asset, it must be recorded within an account classification. Account classifications are used to aggregate fixed assets into groups, so that the same depreciation methods and useful lives can be applied to them.

You also usually create general ledger accounts by classification, and store fixed asset transactions within the classifications to which they belong. Here are the most common classifications used:

- *Buildings*. This account may include the cost of acquiring a building, or the cost of constructing one. If the purchase price of a building includes the cost of land, apportion some of the cost to the Land account (which is not depreciated). A large part of the assets associated with a casino will appear in this account.
- *Computer equipment*. This classification can include a broad array of computer equipment, such as routers, servers, and backup power generators. It is useful to set the capitalization limit higher than the cost of desktop and

laptop computers, so that an excessive number of these assets are not tracked.

- *Gaming equipment*. This category includes gaming tables and slot machines.
- *Furniture and fixtures*. This is one of the broadest categories of fixed assets, since it can include many types of office furniture, casino furniture, and room furnishings.
- *Intangible assets*. This is a non-physical asset, examples of which are gaming licenses, trademarks, customer lists and patented technology.
- *Land*. This is the only asset that is not depreciated, because it is considered to have an indeterminate useful life. Include in this category all expenditures to prepare land for its intended purpose, such as demolishing an existing building or grading the land.
- *Land improvements*. Include any expenditures that add functionality to a parcel of land, such as irrigation systems, fencing, and landscaping.
- *Leasehold improvements*. These are improvements to leased space that are made by the tenant, and typically include office space, air conditioning, telephone wiring, and related permanent fixtures.
- *Office equipment*. This account contains such equipment as copiers, printers, and video equipment. Some companies elect to merge this classification into the furniture and fixtures classification, especially if they have few office equipment items.
- *Software*. Includes larger types of departmental or company-wide software, such as a reservations system, gaming system, or accounting software. Many desktop software packages are not sufficiently expensive to exceed the corporate capitalization limit.
- *Vehicles*. This account contains automobiles, vans, and similar types of rolling stock.

Tip: Do not create too many sub-classifications of fixed assets, such as automobiles, vans, light trucks, and heavy trucks within the main "vehicles" classification. If the classification system is too finely divided, there will inevitably be some "crossover" assets that could fall into several classifications. Also, having a large number of classifications requires extra tracking work by the accountant.

EXAMPLE

Break the Bank Casino decides to construct a new casino in an especially parched area of the Nevada desert. It purchases land for $3 million, updates the land with irrigation systems for $400,000, and constructs a hotel and casino for $10 million. It then purchases gaming equipment for $800,000, and furniture and fixtures for $300,000. It aggregates these purchases into the following fixed asset classifications:

Expenditure Item	Classification	Useful Life	Depreciation Method
Building - $10 million	Building	30 years	Straight line
Furniture and fixtures - $300,000	Furniture and fixtures	7 years	Straight line
Irrigation - $400,000	Land improvements	15 years	Straight line
Land - $3 million	Land	Indeterminate	None
Gaming equipment - $800,000	Gaming equipment	5 years	Straight line

Tip: The local government that charges a company a personal property tax may require that the business complete its tax forms using certain asset classifications. It may make sense to contact the government to see which classifications under which it wants the company to report, and adopt these classifications as the company's official classification system. By doing so, it will not be necessary to re-aggregate assets for personal property tax reporting.

Accounting for Fixed Assets

There are several key points in the life of a fixed asset that require recognition in the accounting records; these are the initial recordation of the asset, the recognition of depreciation, and the eventual derecognition of the asset. Depending on the circumstances, there may also be an asset impairment. We describe these general concepts in the following bullet points:

- *Initial recognition.* There are a number of factors to consider when initially recording a fixed asset, such as the base unit, which costs to include, and when to stop capitalizing costs.
- *Depreciation.* The cost of a fixed asset is gradually charged to expense over time, using depreciation. There are a variety of depreciation methods available, which are described in later sections.
- *Impairment.* There are numerous circumstances under which an asset's recorded value is considered to be impaired. If so, the value of the asset is written down on the books of the casino.
- *Derecognition.* When an asset comes to the end of its useful life, a casino will likely sell or otherwise dispose of it. At this time, remove it from the accounting records, as well as record a gain or loss (if any) on the final disposal transaction.

The Capitalization Limit

One of the most important decisions to be made in the initial recognition of a fixed asset is what minimum cost level to use, below which an expenditure is recorded as an expense in the period incurred, rather than as a fixed asset. This capitalization limit, which is frequently abbreviated as the *cap limit*, is usually driven by the following factors:

- *Asset tracking*. If an expenditure is recorded as a fixed asset, the fixed asset tracking system may impose a significant amount of control over the newly-recorded fixed asset. This can be good, if you want to know where an asset is at any time. Conversely, there is not usually a tracking system in place for an expenditure that is charged to expense, since the assumption is that such items are consumed at once, and so require no subsequent tracking.
- *Fixed asset volume*. The number of expenditures that will be recorded as fixed assets will increase dramatically as the cap limit is lowered. For example, there may only be one fixed asset if the cap limit is $100,000, 50 assets if the cap limit is $10,000, and 500 assets if the cap limit is $1,000. Analyze historical expenditures to estimate a cap limit that will prevent the accountant from being deluged with additional fixed asset records.
- *Profit pressure*. Senior management may have a strong interest in reporting the highest possible profit levels right now, which means that they want a very low cap limit that shifts as many expenditures as possible into capitalized assets. Since this pressure can result in a vast number of very low-cost fixed assets, this issue can create a considerable work load for the accountant.
- *Record keeping*. The accountant can spend a considerable amount of time tracking fixed assets, formulating depreciation, and eliminating fixed assets from the records once they have been disposed of. This can be quite a burden if there are a large number of assets.
- *Tax requirements*. Some government entities require a business to report fixed assets, so that they can charge a personal property tax that is calculated from the reported fixed asset levels. Clearly, a high cap limit will reduce the number of reported fixed assets, and therefore the tax paid. However, government entities may require a minimum cap limit in order to protect their tax revenues.

From an efficiency or tax liability perspective, a high cap limit is always best, since it greatly reduces the work of the accountant and results in lower personal property taxes. From a profitability or asset tracking perspective, you would want the reverse, with a very low cap limit. These conflicting objectives call for some discussion within the management team about the most appropriate cap limit – it should not simply be imposed on the company by the accountant.

The Base Unit

There is no specific guidance in the accounting standards about the unit of measure for a fixed asset. This unit of measure, or *base unit*, is essentially a company's definition of what constitutes a fixed asset. This definition can be formalized into a policy, so that it is applied consistently over time. Here are several issues to consider when creating a definition of a base unit:

- *Aggregation.* Should individually insignificant items be aggregated into a fixed asset, such as a group of gaming tables? This increases the administrative burden, but does delay recognition of the expense associated with the items.

> **Tip:** If the company is billed by a supplier for several assets on a single invoice, do not record everything on the invoice as a single fixed asset. Instead, determine the base unit for each asset, and allocate the freight and tax for the entire invoice to the individual fixed assets that you choose to recognize.

- *Component replacement.* Is it likely that large components of an asset will be replaced during its useful life? If so, designate the smaller units as the most appropriate base unit to track in the accounting records. This decision may be influenced by the probability of these smaller components actually being replaced over time. For example, the roof of a casino could be designated as a separate asset, since it may be replaced several times over the life of the building.
- *Identification.* Can you identify an asset that has been designated as a base unit, or at least attach an asset tag to it? If not, you will not be able to subsequently track it, and so should not designate it as a base unit. This is a common problem in an adjoining hotel that may invest in dozens or hundreds of identical beds, chairs, and side tables.
- *Legal description.* If there is a legal description of an asset, such as is stated on a tax billing for a specific parcel of land, this can form the basis for a base unit, since you can then associate future expenses billed by a government entity to the base unit.
- *Tax treatment.* Is there a tax advantage in separately accounting for the components of a major asset? This may be the case where the useful life of a component is shorter than that of a major asset of which it is a part, so that it can be depreciated quicker.
- *Useful life.* The useful lives of the components of a base unit should be similar, so that the entire unit can be eliminated or replaced at approximately the same time.

EXAMPLE

Treasure Chest Casino operates facilities located in areas that are subject to major hailstorms, which commonly result in hail damage to roofs. On average, hail damage will require the replacement of a roof every ten years, while the rest of each casino structure is estimated to be viable for at least 50 years. Given these differences, it makes sense for the company to designate the roofs as separate base units.

The Initial Measurement of a Fixed Asset

Initially record a fixed asset at the historical cost of acquiring it, which includes the costs to bring it to the condition and location necessary for its intended use. If these preparatory activities will occupy a period of time, also include in the cost of the asset the interest costs related to the cost of the asset during the preparation period. The treatment of interest costs is addressed in the following Interest Capitalization chapter.

The activities involved in bringing a fixed asset to the condition and location necessary for its intended purpose include the following:

- Physical construction of the asset
- Demolition of any preexisting structures
- Renovating a preexisting structure to alter it for use by the buyer
- Administrative and technical activities during preconstruction for such activities as designing the asset and obtaining permits
- Administrative and technical work after construction commences for such activities as litigation, labor disputes, and technical problems

EXAMPLE

A casino decides to add an additional air conditioning unit to its main casino area, which involves the creation of a concrete pad for the unit, stringing electrical cabling to it, linking it to the building's air conditioning vents, and obtaining an electrical permit. All of the following costs can be included in the fixed asset cost of the unit:

Air conditioning unit price	$120,000
Concrete pad	3,000
Wiring and ducts	5,000
Electrical permit	200
Total	$128,200

The Purpose of Depreciation

The purpose of depreciation is to charge to expense a portion of an asset that relates to the revenue generated by that asset. This is called the matching principle, where revenues and expenses both appear in the income statement in the same reporting period, which gives the best view of how well a company has performed in a given accounting period. The trouble with this matching concept is that there is usually only a tenuous connection between the generation of revenue and a specific asset.

To get around this linkage problem, we usually assume a steady rate of depreciation over the useful life of each asset, so that we approximate a linkage between the recognition of revenues and expenses. This approximation threatens our credulity even more when a company uses accelerated depreciation, since the main reason for using it is to defer taxes (and not to better match revenues and expenses).

If we were not to use depreciation at all, we would be forced to charge all assets to expense as soon as we buy them. This would result in large losses in the months when this purchase transaction occurs, followed by unusually high profitability in those periods when the corresponding amount of revenue is recognized, with no offsetting expense. Thus, a company that does not use depreciation will have front-loaded expenses, and extremely variable financial results.

Depreciation Concepts

There are three factors to consider in the calculation of depreciation, which are as follows:

- *Useful life.* This is the time period over which it is expected that an asset will be productive, or the amount of activity expected to be generated by it. Past its useful life, it is no longer cost-effective to continue operating the asset, so the company would dispose of it or stop using it. Depreciation is recognized over the useful life of an asset.

Tip: Rather than recording a different useful life for every asset, it is easier to assign each asset to an asset class, where every asset in that asset class has the same useful life. This approach may not work for very high-cost assets, where a greater degree of precision may be needed.

- *Salvage value.* When a company eventually disposes of an asset, it may be able to sell the asset for some reduced amount, which is the salvage value. Depreciation is calculated based on the asset cost, less any estimated salvage value. If salvage value is expected to be quite small, it is generally ignored for the purpose of calculating depreciation.

EXAMPLE

The Treasure Chest Casino buys a shuttle van for $75,000, and estimates that its salvage value will be $15,000 in five years, when it plans to dispose of the asset. This means that Treasure Chest will depreciate $60,000 of the asset cost over five years, leaving $15,000 of the cost remaining at the end of that time. The casino expects to then sell the asset for $15,000, which will eliminate the asset from its accounting records.

- *Depreciation method.* Depreciation expense can be calculated using an accelerated depreciation method, or evenly over the useful life of the asset. The advantage of using an accelerated method is that a business can recognize more depreciation early in the life of a fixed asset, which defers some income tax expense recognition to a later period. The advantage of using a steady depreciation rate is the ease of calculation. Examples of accelerated depreciation methods are the double declining balance and sum-of-the-years' digits methods. The primary method for steady depreciation is the straight-line method.

The *mid-month convention* states that, no matter when a fixed asset is purchased in a month, it is assumed to have been purchased in the middle of the month for depreciation purposes. Thus, if a fixed asset was purchased on January 5th, assume that it was bought on January 15th; or, if it was acquired on January 28, still assume that it was bought on January 15th. By doing so, it is easier to calculate a standard half-month of depreciation for the first month of ownership.

If you choose to use the mid-month convention, this also means that you should record a half-month of depreciation for the *last* month of the asset's useful life. By doing so, the two half-month depreciation calculations equal one full month of depreciation.

Many companies prefer to use full-month depreciation in the first month of ownership, irrespective of the actual date of purchase within the month, so that they can slightly accelerate their recognition of depreciation, which in turn reduces their taxable income in the near term.

Accelerated Depreciation

Accelerated depreciation is the depreciation of fixed assets at a very fast rate early in their useful lives. The primary reason for using accelerated depreciation is to reduce the reported amount of taxable income over the first few years of an asset's life, so that a company pays a smaller amount of income taxes during those early years. Later on, when most of the depreciation will have already been recognized, the effect reverses, so there will be less depreciation available to shelter taxable income. The result is that a company pays more income taxes in later years. Thus, the net effect of accelerated depreciation is the deferral of income taxes to later time periods.

A secondary reason for using accelerated depreciation is that it may actually reflect the usage pattern of the underlying assets, where they experience heavy usage early in their useful lives.

There are several calculations available for accelerated depreciation, such as the double declining balance method and the sum of the years' digits method. We will describe these methods in the following sub-sections.

All of the depreciation methods end up recognizing the same amount of depreciation, which is the cost of the fixed asset less any expected salvage value. The only difference between the various methods is the speed with which depreciation is recognized.

Accelerated depreciation requires additional depreciation calculations and record keeping, so some companies avoid it for that reason (though fixed asset software can readily overcome this issue). They may also ignore it if they are not consistently earning taxable income, which takes away the primary reason for using it. Companies may also ignore accelerated depreciation if they have a relatively small amount of fixed assets, so that the tax effect of using accelerated depreciation is minimal.

Sum-of-the-Years' Digits Method

The sum of the years' digits (SYD) method is used to calculate depreciation on an accelerated basis. Use the following formula to calculate it:

$$\text{Depreciation percentage} = \frac{\text{Number of estimated years of life as of beginning of the year}}{\text{Sum of the years' digits}}$$

The following table contains examples of the sum of the years' digits noted in the denominator of the preceding formula:

Total Depreciation Period	Initial Sum of the Years' Digits	Calculation
2 years	3	1 + 2
3 years	6	1 + 2 + 3
4 years	10	1 + 2 + 3 + 4
5 years	15	1 + 2 + 3 + 4 + 5

The concept is illustrated in the following example.

EXAMPLE

Executive Casinos buys a slot machine for $10,000. The machine has no estimated salvage value, and a useful life of five years. Executive calculates the annual sum of the years' digits depreciation for this machine as:

Year	Number of estimated years of life as of beginning of the year	SYD Calculation	Depreciation Percentage	Annual Depreciation
1	5	5/15	33.33%	$3,333
2	4	4/15	26.67%	2,667
3	3	3/15	20.00%	2,000
4	2	2/15	13.33%	1,333
5	1	1/15	6.67%	667
Totals	15		100.00%	$10,000

Double-Declining Balance Method

The double declining balance (DDB) method is a form of accelerated depreciation. To calculate the double-declining balance depreciation rate, divide the number of years of useful life of an asset into 100 percent, and multiply the result by two. The formula is:

$$(100\% \div \text{Years of useful life}) \times 2$$

The DDB calculation proceeds until the asset's salvage value is reached, after which depreciation ends.

EXAMPLE

The Money Casino purchases a small airport van for $50,000. It has an estimated salvage value of $5,000 and a useful life of five years. The calculation of the double declining balance depreciation rate is:

$$(100\% \div \text{Years of useful life}) \times 2 = 40\%$$

By applying the 40% rate, Money arrives at the following table of depreciation charges per year:

Year	Book Value at Beginning of Year	Depreciation Percentage	DDB Depreciation	Book Value Net of Depreciation
1	$50,000	40%	$20,000	$30,000
2	30,000	40%	12,000	18,000
3	18,000	40%	7,200	10,800
4	10,800	40%	4,320	6,480
5	6,480	40%	1,480	5,000
Total			$45,000	

Note that the depreciation in the fifth and final year is only for $1,480, rather than the $3,240 that would be indicated by the 40% depreciation rate. The reason for the smaller depreciation charge is that Money stops any further depreciation once the remaining book value declines to the amount of the estimated salvage value.

Straight-Line Method

If a company elects not to use accelerated depreciation, it can instead use the straight-line method, where it depreciates an asset at the same standard rate throughout its useful life. Under the straight-line method of depreciation, recognize depreciation expense evenly over the estimated useful life of an asset. The straight-line calculation steps are:

1. Subtract the estimated salvage value of the asset from the amount at which it is recorded on the books.
2. Determine the estimated useful life of the asset. It is easiest to use a standard useful life for each class of assets.
3. Divide the estimated useful life (in years) into 1 to arrive at the straight-line depreciation rate.
4. Multiply the depreciation rate by the asset cost (less salvage value).

EXAMPLE

The Energetic Casino's buffet restaurant purchases a Grill Master Deluxe machine for $6,000. It has an estimated salvage value of $1,000 and a useful life of five years. Energetic calculates the annual straight-line depreciation for the grill as:
1. Purchase cost of $6,000 – Estimated salvage value of $1,000 = Depreciable asset cost of $5,000
2. 1 ÷ 5-Year useful life = 20% Depreciation rate per year
3. 20% Depreciation rate × $5,000 Depreciable asset cost = $1,000 Annual depreciation

---

Units of Activity Method

Under the units of activity method, the amount of depreciation charged to expense varies in direct proportion to the amount of asset usage. Thus, more depreciation is charged in periods when there is more asset usage, and less depreciation in periods when there is less asset usage. It is the most accurate method for charging depreciation, since it links closely to the wear and tear on assets. However, it also requires the tracking of asset usage, which means that its use is generally limited to more expensive assets. Also, you need to estimate total usage over the life of the asset.

Tip: Do not use the units of activity method if there is not a significant difference in asset usage from period to period. Otherwise, you will spend a great deal of time tracking asset usage, and will be rewarded with a depreciation expense that varies little from the results that would have been experienced with the straight-line method (which is far easier to calculate).

Follow these steps to calculate depreciation under the units of activity method:
1. Estimate the total number of hours of usage of the asset, or the total amount of activity to be produced by it over its useful life.
2. Subtract any estimated salvage value from the capitalized cost of the asset, and divide the total estimated usage from this net depreciable cost. This yields the depreciation cost per hour of usage or other unit of activity.
3. Multiply the number of hours of usage or units of actual activity by the depreciation cost per hour or unit of activity, which results in the total depreciation expense for the accounting period.

118

If the estimated number of hours of usage or units of activity changes over time, incorporate these changes into the calculation of the depreciation cost per hour or unit of activity. This will alter the depreciation expense on a go-forward basis.

EXAMPLE

The Fabulous Casino has just purchased a passenger van that it uses to provide shuttle service to the local airport. The cost of the van was $90,000. The casino manager expects to use the van for 50,000 miles and then sell it off at a salvage value of $40,000, which leaves $50,000 to be depreciated. Since van usage depends on passenger traffic to the airport, and that traffic depends on customer demand, the manager elects to use the units of activity method for depreciation. Accordingly, the depreciation rate is set at $1 per mile traveled (calculated as $50,000 to be depreciated ÷ 50,000 miles). During the first month of operation, Fabulous runs the van for 650 miles, and so charges $650 to depreciation expense.

The Depreciation of Land

Nearly all fixed assets have a useful life, after which they no longer contribute to the operations of a company or they stop generating revenue. During this useful life, they are depreciated, which reduces their cost to what they are supposed to be worth at the end of their useful lives. Land, however, has no definitive useful life, so there is no way to depreciate it.

The Depreciation of Land Improvements

Land improvements are enhancements to a plot of land to make it more usable. If these improvements have a useful life, depreciate them. If there is no way to estimate a useful life, do not depreciate the cost of the improvements.

If you are preparing land for its intended purpose, include these costs in the cost of the land asset. They are not depreciated. Examples of such costs are:
- Demolishing an existing building
- Clearing and leveling the land

If functionality is being added to the land and the expenditures have a useful life, record them in a separate Land Improvements account. Examples of land improvements are:
- Drainage and irrigation systems
- Fencing
- Landscaping
- Parking lots and walkways

A special item is the ongoing cost of landscaping. This is a period cost, not a fixed asset, and so should be charged to expense as incurred.

EXAMPLE

Quest Casino buys a parcel of land for $1,000,000. Since it is a purchase of land, Quest cannot depreciate the cost. Quest then razes a building that was located on the property at a cost of $25,000, fills in the old foundation for $5,000, and levels the land for $50,000. All of these costs are to prepare the land for its intended purpose, so they are all added to the cost of the land. Quest cannot depreciate these costs.

Quest intends to use the land as a parking lot for the casino, so it spends $350,000 to create a parking lot. It estimates that these improvements have a useful life of 10 years. It should record this cost in the Land Improvements account, and depreciate it over 10 years.

Depreciation Accounting Entries

The basic depreciation entry is to debit the depreciation expense account (which appears in the income statement) and credit the accumulated depreciation account (which appears in the balance sheet as a contra account that reduces the amount of fixed assets). Over time, the accumulated depreciation balance will continue to increase as more depreciation is added to it, until such time as it equals the original cost of the asset. At that time, stop recording any depreciation expense, since the cost of the asset has now been reduced to zero.

The journal entry for depreciation can be a simple two-line entry designed to accommodate all types of fixed assets, or it may be subdivided into separate entries for each type of fixed asset.

EXAMPLE

Quest Casino calculates that it should have $25,000 of depreciation expense in the current month. The entry is:

	Debit	Credit
Depreciation expense	25,000	
Accumulated depreciation		25,000

In the following month, Quest's accountant decides to show a higher level of precision at the expense account level, and instead elects to apportion the $25,000 of depreciation among different expense accounts, so that each class of asset has a separate depreciation charge.

The entry is:

	Debit	Credit
Depreciation expense – Automobiles	4,000	
Depreciation expense – Gaming equipment	8,000	
Depreciation expense – Furniture and fixtures	6,000	
Depreciation expense – Office equipment	5,000	
Depreciation expense – Software	2,000	
Accumulated depreciation		25,000

Accumulated Depreciation

When an asset is sold or otherwise disposed of, remove all related accumulated depreciation from the accounting records at the same time. Otherwise, an unusually large amount of accumulated depreciation will build up on the balance sheet.

EXAMPLE

Quest Casino has $1,000,000 of fixed assets, for which it has charged $380,000 of accumulated depreciation. This results in the following presentation on Quest's balance sheet:

Fixed assets	$1,000,000
Less: Accumulated depreciation	(380,000)
Net fixed assets	$620,000

Quest then sells equipment for $80,000 that had an original cost of $140,000, and for which it had already recorded accumulated depreciation of $50,000. It records the sale with this journal entry:

	Debit	Credit
Cash	80,000	
Accumulated depreciation	50,000	
Loss on asset sale	10,000	
Fixed assets		140,000

As a result of this entry, Quest's balance sheet presentation of fixed assets has changed, so that fixed assets before accumulated depreciation have declined to $860,000, and accumulated depreciation has declined to $330,000. The new presentation is:

Fixed assets	$860,000
Less: Accumulated depreciation	(330,000)
Net fixed assets	$530,000

The amount of net fixed assets declined by $90,000 as a result of the asset sale, which is the sum of the $80,000 cash proceeds and the $10,000 loss resulting from the asset sale.

Asset Impairment

A casino has a massive investment in assets, and so is at increased risk of being required to record a large loss on the value of those assets, which is called an impairment loss. This section describes the key features of the rules related to asset impairment. There are a number of sub-headings listed, since this is a significant topic that covers a large number of areas related to impairment.

Measurement of Asset Impairment

An impairment loss on a fixed asset is recognized if its carrying amount is not recoverable and exceeds its fair value. *Carrying amount* is the original acquisition cost of an asset, less any subsequent depreciation and impairment charges.

The carrying amount of an asset is not recoverable if it exceeds the sum of the undiscounted cash flows expected to result from the use of the asset over its remaining useful life and the final disposition of the asset. These cash flow estimates should incorporate assumptions that are reasonable in relation to the assumptions the entity uses for a casino's budgets, forecasts, and so forth. If there are a range of possible cash flow outcomes, consider using a probability-weighted cash flow analysis.

Tip: Base the impairment analysis on the cash flows to be expected over the remaining useful life of the asset. If you are measuring impairment for a group of assets (as discussed below), the remaining useful life is based on the useful life of the primary asset in the group. Do not skew the results by including in the group an asset with a theoretically unlimited life, such as land or an intangible asset that is not being amortized.

The amount of an impairment loss is the difference between an asset's carrying amount and its fair value. Once you recognize an impairment loss, this reduces the carrying amount of the asset, so you may need to alter the amount of periodic depreciation being charged against the asset to adjust for this lower carrying amount (otherwise, you will incur an excessively large depreciation expense over the remaining useful life of the asset).

The Asset to be Tested

Test assets for impairment at the lowest level at which there are identifiable cash flows that are largely independent of the cash flows of other assets. In cases where there are no identifiable cash flows at all (as is common with corporate-level assets), place these assets in an asset group that encompasses the entire entity, and test for impairment at the entity level.

A reporting unit is an operating segment or one level below an operating segment. An operating segment is a component of a public entity that engages in business activities and whose results are reviewed by the chief operating decision maker, and for which discrete financial information is available.

Timing of the Impairment Test

Test for the recoverability of an asset whenever the circumstances indicate that its carrying amount may not be recoverable. Examples of such situations that are specific to a casino are:

- *Costs*. Local labor costs have increased to the point where they are impinging on the cash flows of the casino.
- *Costs*. The cost to construct a casino turns out to be excessively high.
- *Disposal*. There is a more than 50% probability that a slot machine will be sold or otherwise disposed of significantly before the end of its previously estimated useful life.
- *Regulatory*. A casino loses its liquor license.
- *Regulatory*. A gaming license change caps the amount of losses that a player is allowed to sustain.
- *Regulatory*. A gaming license change restricts the types of games that can be played.
- *Regulatory*. A gaming license is awarded to another casino a short distance away.
- *Taxes*. The governing political entity raises the gaming tax rate.
- *Trends*. There is an observable decline in travel to the casino.

Accounting for the Impairment of an Asset Group

If there is an impairment at the level of an asset group, allocate the impairment among the assets in the group on a pro rata basis, based on the carrying amounts of the assets in the group. However, the impairment loss cannot reduce the carrying amount of an asset below its fair value.

> **Tip:** The relevant accounting standard states that you only have to determine the fair value of an asset for this test if it is "determinable without undue cost and effort." Thus, if an outside appraisal would be required to determine fair value, you can likely dispense with this requirement and simply allocate the impairment loss to all of the assets in the group.

EXAMPLE

Pirates Trove Casino operates a small casino for day trippers. The controller considers the entire facility to be a reporting unit, so it conducts an impairment test on the entire operation. The test reveals that a continuing increase in the number of nearby casinos has caused a $2 million impairment charge. The accounting staff allocates the charge to the four assets in the facility as follows:

Asset	Carrying Amount	Proportion of Carrying Amounts	Impairment Allocation	Revised Carrying Amount
Casino building	$8,000,000	67%	$1,340,000	$6,660,000
Restaurant	1,500,000	13%	260,000	1,240,000
Hotel	2,000,000	16%	320,000	1,680,000
Parking garage	500,000	4%	80,000	420,000
Totals	$12,000,000	100%	$2,000,000	$10,000,000

Asset Derecognition

An asset is derecognized upon its disposal, or when no future economic benefits can be expected from its use or disposal. Derecognition can arise from a variety of events, such as an asset's sale, scrapping, or donation. The net effect of asset derecognition is to remove an asset and its associated accumulated depreciation from the balance sheet, as well as to recognize any related gain or loss. The gain or loss on derecognition is calculated as the net disposal proceeds, minus the asset's carrying amount.

The asset disposal form is used to formalize the disposition of assets. Ideally, the purchasing department should be involved in disposals, since it presumably has the most experience in obtaining the best prices for goods. Consequently, a large part of the form is set aside for the use of the purchasing staff, which describes how the asset is disposed of and the amount of funds (if any) received. There is space to state billing information, in case the buyer is to be billed. There is also a separate section containing a checklist of activities that the accountant must complete. A sample of the form is presented next.

Sample Asset Disposal Form

Asset Disposal Form

Asset Tag Number	Asset Serial Number	Current Location

Asset Description

Reason for Disposal

- [ ] No longer usable
- [ ] Past recommended life span
- [ ] Being replaced

- [ ] Being traded in
- [ ] Lost or stolen*
- [ ] Other _____

* Contact building security to file a police report

Department Manager Approval Signature

For Use by Purchasing Department

Type of Disposition

- [ ] Sold ($_____)
- [ ] Donated
- [ ] Scrapped
- [ ] Other _____

If buyer is to be invoiced, state billing information:

Buyer billing information

Purchasing Manager Approval Signature	Disposal Date

For Use by Accounting Department

Accounting Actions Completed

Asset removed from general ledger	Initials	Date
Asset removed from fixed asset register	Initials	Date
Buyer billed for sale amount	Initials	Date
Cash receipt recorded	Initials	Date

Abandoned and Idle Assets

If a company abandons an asset, consider the asset to be disposed of, and account for it as such (even if it remains on the premises). However, if the asset is only temporarily idle, do not consider it to be abandoned, and continue to depreciate it in a normal manner. If an asset has been abandoned, reduce its carrying amount down to any remaining salvage value on the date when the decision is made to abandon the asset.

Some fixed assets will be idle from time to time. There is no specific consideration of idle assets in the accounting standards, so continue to depreciate these assets in the normal manner. However, if an asset is idle, this may indicate that its useful life is shorter than the amount currently used to calculate its depreciation. This may call for a re-evaluation of its useful life.

Asset Disposal Accounting

There are two scenarios under which a business may dispose of a fixed asset. The first situation arises when a fixed asset is being eliminated without receiving any payment in return. This is a common situation when a fixed asset is being scrapped because it is obsolete or no longer in use, and there is no resale market for it. In this case, reverse any accumulated depreciation and reverse the original asset cost. If the asset is fully depreciated, that is the extent of the entry.

EXAMPLE

Quest Casino buys a slot machine for $10,000 and recognizes $1,000 of depreciation per year over the following ten years. At that time, the machine is not only fully depreciated, but also ready for the scrap heap. Quest gives away the machine for free, and records the following entry.

	Debit	Credit
Accumulated depreciation	10,000	
Equipment asset		10,000

A variation on this situation is to write off a fixed asset that has not yet been completely depreciated. In this case, write off the remaining undepreciated amount of the asset to a loss account.

EXAMPLE

To use the same example, Quest gives away the slot machine after eight years, when it has not yet depreciated $2,000 of the asset's original $10,000 cost. In this case, Quest records the following entry:

	Debit	Credit
Loss on asset disposal	2,000	
Accumulated depreciation	8,000	
Equipment asset		10,000

The second scenario arises when an asset is sold, so that the company receives cash in exchange for the fixed asset being sold. Depending upon the price paid and the remaining amount of depreciation that has not yet been charged to expense, this can result in either a gain or a loss on sale of the asset.

EXAMPLE

Quest Casino still disposes of its $10,000 slot machine, but does so after seven years, and sells it for $3,500 in cash. In this case, it has already recorded $7,000 of depreciation expense. The entry is:

	Debit	Credit
Cash	3,500	
Accumulated depreciation	7,000	
Gain on asset disposal		500
Equipment asset		10,000

What if Quest had sold the machine for $2,500 instead of $3,500? Then there would be a loss of $500 on the sale. The entry would be:

	Debit	Credit
Cash	2,500	
Accumulated depreciation	7,000	
Loss on asset disposal	500	
Machine asset		10,000

The "loss on asset disposal" or "gain on asset disposal" accounts noted in the preceding sample entries are called disposal accounts. They may be combined into a single account or used separately to store gains and losses resulting from the disposal of fixed assets.

Slot Participation Agreements

A unique aspect of casinos is the manner in which they obtain slot machines. They could pay a fixed price for a machine, or they could lease it. A third option is that the slot manufacturer and the casino can agree to a revenue sharing agreement, where the manufacturer installs a slot machine in the casino, and is paid a proportion of the revenues, such as 20%. Alternatively, the casino could pay the manufacturer a percentage of the *coin-in* on the machine. Coin-in is the amount paid into the machine by customers. This is essentially a variable lease payment, where the manufacturer retains ownership of the slot machine. From the perspective of the casino, these arrangements are operating leases, so they do not record the slot machines as assets, nor do they recognize any depreciation expense. Thus, the casino still records the full amount of all slot machine winnings as revenue, while also charging the payments made to the machine manufacturer to expense.

A slot participation arrangement is especially common for locations hosting a small number of slot machines, such as a bar. A slot machine route operator owns the slot machines, and services them on a regular maintenance run, as would be the case with vending machines. Such an agreement may also be used for an unusual slot machine that casino management is not willing to purchase until it tests the unit's profit-making potential, so it instead commits to a slot participation agreement for a short period of time. If the machine performs, then management may buy the machine.

Summary

From the perspective of the accountant, the tracking of fixed assets can be quite time-consuming. Consequently, we recommend setting a high capitalization limit in order to charge most purchases to expense at once, rather than recording them as fixed assets.

Depreciation is one of the central concerns of the accountant, since the broad range of available methods can result in significant differences in the amount of depreciation expense recorded in each period. Generally, adopt the straight-line depreciation method to minimize the amount of depreciation calculations, unless the usage rate of the assets involved more closely matches a different depreciation method.

> **Tip:** Use the straight-line depreciation method whenever possible, because it is easier for outside auditors to verify these calculations. This may lead to a small reduction in audit fees.

Chapter 7
Interest Capitalization

Introduction

A capital project may be created in order to separately track the creation of a large asset, such as a casino/hotel/parking garage complex. If a company incurs debt to build such an asset, it should capitalize the interest expense associated with the asset. The accountant should know the rules for capitalizing interest, which are discussed in this chapter.

Overview of Capitalized Interest

Interest is a cost of doing business, and if a company incurs an interest cost that is directly related to an asset, it is reasonable to capitalize this cost, since it provides a truer picture of the total investment in the asset. Since a business would not otherwise have incurred the interest if it had not acquired the asset, the interest is essentially a direct cost of owning the asset.

Conversely, if a business does not capitalize this interest cost and instead charges it to expense, the entity would be unreasonably reducing the amount of reported earnings during the period when the company incurred the expense, and increasing earnings during later periods, when it would otherwise have been charging the capitalized interest to expense through depreciation.

> **Tip:** If the amount of interest that may be applied to an asset is minor, try to avoid capitalizing it. Otherwise, you will spend extra time documenting the capitalization, and the auditors will spend time investigating it – which may translate into higher audit fees.

The value of the information provided by capitalizing interest may not be worth the effort of the incremental accounting cost associated with it. Here are some issues to consider when deciding whether to capitalize interest:

- How many assets would be subject to interest capitalization?
- How easy is it to separately identify those assets that would be subject to interest capitalization?
- How significant would be the effect of interest capitalization on the company's reported resources and earnings?

Thus, only capitalize interest when the informational benefit derived from doing so exceeds the cost of accounting for it. The positive impact of doing so is greatest for construction projects, where:

- Costs are separately compiled

Interest Capitalization

- Construction covers a long period of time
- Expenditures are large
- Interest costs are considerable

When to Capitalize Interest

A casino should capitalize interest on assets that are constructed for its own use. This includes assets built for the company by suppliers, where the company makes progress payments or deposits.

EXAMPLE

The Morton Hotels chain decides to build a casino/hotel complex in downtown Las Vegas. The company hires a contractor to perform the work, and makes regular progress payments to the contractor. Morton should capitalize the interest expense related to this project.

If a company is undertaking activities to develop land for a specific use, capitalize interest related to the associated expenditures for as long as the development activities are in progress.

Do not capitalize interest that is related to the following types of fixed assets:

- Assets that are already in use or ready for their intended use
- Assets not being used, and which are not being prepared for use
- Assets not included in the company's balance sheet

The Interest Capitalization Period

Capitalize interest over the period when there are ongoing activities to prepare a fixed asset for its intended use, but only if expenditures are actually being made during that time, and interest costs are being incurred.

EXAMPLE

The Pirates Casino is constructing an in-house staff training facility. It spent the first two months designing the layout, and then paid a contractor $30,000 per month for the next four months to build the facility. Pirates incurred interest costs during the entire time period.

Since Pirates was not making any expenditures related to the training facility during the first two months, it cannot capitalize any interest cost for those two months. However, since it was making expenditures during the next four months, it can capitalize interest cost for those months.

If a company stops essentially all construction on a project, stop capitalizing interest during that period. However, continue to capitalize interest under any of the following circumstances:

130

- Brief construction interruptions
- Interruptions imposed by an outside entity
- Delays that are an inherent part of the asset acquisition process

---

EXAMPLE

Penny-Pinching Casinos is constructing a day trippers casino. Midway through the project, the local municipality orders a halt to all construction, when construction reveals that the complex is being built on an Indian burial ground. Two months later, after the burial site has been relocated, the municipality allows construction to begin again.

Since this interruption was imposed by an outside entity, the casino can capitalize interest during the two-month stoppage period.

A company should terminate interest capitalization as soon as an asset is substantially complete and ready for its intended use. Here are several scenarios showing when to terminate interest capitalization:

- *Unit-level completion.* Parts of a project may be completed and usable before the entire project is complete. Stop capitalizing interest on each of these parts as soon as they are substantially complete and ready for use.
- *Entire-unit completion.* All aspects of an asset may need to be completed before any part of it can be used. Continue capitalizing interest on such assets until the entire project is substantially complete and ready for use.
- *Dependent completion.* An asset may not be usable until a separate project has also been completed. Continue capitalizing interest on such assets until not only the specific asset, but also the separate project is substantially complete and ready for use.

EXAMPLE

Pirates Casinos is building two gambling facilities, both under different circumstances. They are:

1. *Project A.* This is a casino with an integrated multi-level parking garage. Even though the garage is completed first, Pirates should continue to capitalize interest for it, since the garage is only intended to service patrons of the casino, and so will not be operational until the casino is complete.
2. *Project B.* This a gambling and lodging complex for which Pirates is also constructing a highway off-ramp and road that leads to the complex. Since the complex is unusable until patrons can reach the complex, Pirates should continue to capitalize interest expenses until the off-ramp and road are complete.

Do not continue to capitalize interest when completion is being deliberately delayed, since the cost of interest then changes from an asset acquisition cost to an asset holding cost.

EXAMPLE

The CEO of Pirates Casinos wants to report increased net income for the upcoming quarter, so he orders the delay of construction on a casino that would otherwise have been completed, so that the interest cost related to the project will be capitalized. He is in error, since this is now treated as a holding cost – the related interest expense should be recognized in the period incurred, rather than capitalized.

The Capitalization Rate

The amount of interest cost to capitalize for a fixed asset is that amount of interest that would have been avoided if the company had not acquired the asset. To calculate the amount of interest cost to capitalize, multiply the capitalization rate by the average amount of expenditures that accumulate during the construction period.

The basis for the capitalization rate is the interest rates that are applicable to the company's borrowings that are outstanding during the construction period. If a specific borrowing is incurred in order to construct a specific asset, use the interest rate on that borrowing as the capitalization rate. If the amount of a specific borrowing that is incurred to construct a specific asset is less than the expenditures made for the asset, use a weighted average of the rates applicable to other company borrowings for any excess expenditures over the amount of the project-specific borrowing.

EXAMPLE

Pirates Casinos incurs an average expenditure over the construction period of a casino of $15,000,000. It has taken out a short-term loan of $12,000,000 at 9% interest specifically to cover the cost of this project. Pirates can capitalize the interest cost of the entire amount of the $12,000,000 loan at 9% interest, but it still has $3,000,000 of average expenditures that exceed the amount of this project-specific loan.

Pirates has two bonds outstanding at the time of the project, in the following amounts:

Bond Description	Principal Outstanding	Interest
8% Bond	$18,000,000	$1,440,000
10% Bond	12,000,000	1,200,000
Totals	$30,000,000	$2,640,000

The weighted-average interest rate on these two bond issuances is 8.8% ($2,640,000 interest ÷ $30,000,000 principal), which is the interest rate that Pirates should use when capitalizing the remaining $3,000,000 of average expenditures.

These rules regarding the formulation of the capitalization rate are subject to some interpretation. The key guideline is to arrive at a *reasonable* measure of the cost of

132

financing the acquisition of a fixed asset, particularly in regard to the interest cost that could have been avoided if the acquisition had not been made. Thus, it is possible to use a selection of outstanding borrowings as the basis for a weighted average calculation. This may result in the inclusion or exclusion of borrowings at the corporate level, or just at the level of the subsidiary where the asset is located.

EXAMPLE

Executive Casinos has issued several bonds and notes, totaling $50,000,000, that are used to fund both general corporate activities and construction projects. It also has access to a low-cost 4% internal line of credit that is extended to it by its corporate parent, Executive International. Executive Casinos regularly uses this line of credit for short-term activities, and typically draws the balance down to zero at least once a year. The average amount of this line that is outstanding is approximately $10,000,000 at any given time.

Since the corporate line of credit comprises a significant amount of Executive Casino's ongoing borrowings, and there is no restriction that prevents these funds from being used for construction projects, it would be reasonable to include the interest cost of this line of credit in the calculation of the weighted-average cost of borrowings that is used to derive its capitalization rate.

Calculating Interest Capitalization

Follow these steps to calculate the amount of interest to be capitalized for a specific project:
1. Construct a table itemizing the amounts of expenditures made and the dates on which the expenditures were made.
2. Determine the date on which interest capitalization ends.
3. Calculate the capitalization period for each expenditure, which is the number of days between the specific expenditure and the end of the interest capitalization period.
4. Divide each capitalization period by the total number of days elapsed between the date of the first expenditure and the end of the interest capitalization period to arrive at the capitalization multiplier for each line item.
5. Multiply each expenditure amount by its capitalization multiplier to arrive at the average expenditure for each line item over the capitalization measurement period.
6. Add up the average expenditures at the line item level to arrive at a grand total average expenditure.
7. If there is project-specific debt, multiply the grand total of the average expenditures by the interest rate on that debt to arrive at the capitalized interest related to that debt.
8. If the grand total of the average expenditures exceeds the amount of the project-specific debt, multiply the excess expenditure amount by the

weighted average of the company's other outstanding debt to arrive at the remaining amount of interest to be capitalized.

9. Add together both capitalized interest calculations. If the combined total is more than the total interest cost incurred by the company during the calculation period, reduce the amount of interest to be capitalized to the total interest cost incurred by the company during the calculation period.

10. Record the interest capitalization with a debit to the project's fixed asset account and a credit to the interest expense account.

EXAMPLE

Money Casinos is building a new casino facility. Money makes payments related to the project of $10,000,000 and $14,000,000 to a contractor on January 1 and July 1, respectively. The casino is completed on December 31.

For the 12-month period of construction, Money can capitalize all of the interest on the $10,000,000 payment, since it was outstanding during the full period of construction. Money can capitalize the interest on the $14,000,000 payment for half of the construction period, since it was outstanding during only the second half of the construction period. The average expenditure for which the interest cost can be capitalized is calculated in the following table:

Date of Payment	Expenditure Amount	Capitalization Period*	Capitalization Multiplier	Average Expenditure
January 1	$10,000,000	12 months	12/12 months = 100%	$10,000,000
July 1	14,000,000	6 months	6/12 months = 50%	7,000,000
				$17,000,000

* In the table, the capitalization period is defined as the number of months that elapse between the expenditure payment date and the end of the interest capitalization period.

The only debt that Money has outstanding during this period is a line of credit, on which the interest rate is 8%. The maximum amount of interest that Money can capitalize into the cost of this project is $1,360,000, which is calculated as:

8% Interest rate × $17,000,000 Average expenditure = $1,360,000

Money records the following journal entry:

	Debit	Credit
Fixed assets – casino	1,360,000	
Interest expense		1,360,000

Tip: There may be an inordinate number of expenditures related to a larger project, which could result in a large and unwieldy calculation of average expenditures. To reduce the workload, consider aggregating these expenses by month, and then assume that each expenditure was made in the middle of the month, thereby reducing all of the expenditures for each month to a single line item.

It is not allowable to capitalize more interest cost in an accounting period than the total amount of interest cost incurred by the business in that period. If there is a corporate parent, this rule means that the amount capitalized cannot exceed the total amount of interest cost incurred by the business on a consolidated basis.

Summary

The key issue with interest capitalization is whether to use it at all. It requires a certain amount of administrative effort to compile, and so is not recommended for lower-value assets. Instead, reserve its use for larger projects where including the cost of interest in an asset will improve the quality of the financial information reported by the entity. It should *not* be used merely to delay the recognition of interest expense. If the choice is made to use interest capitalization, adopt a procedure for determining the amount to be capitalized and closely adhere to it, with appropriate documentation of the results. This will result in a standardized calculation methodology that auditors can more easily review.

Chapter 8
Debt Accounting

Introduction

The investors in a casino may choose to obtain debt financing to help start or fund the business. Doing so can boost their return on investment, if the amount of profit generated by the entity exceeds the amount of interest expense associated with the debt.

The accounting for debt is not especially difficult, especially when there are only a few loans outstanding. Also, the accounting entries needed are fairly simple. However, it is necessary to determine the interest component of each debt payment, so that the borrower properly presents in its balance sheet the correct amount of remaining debt outstanding.

In this chapter, we address the classification of and accounting for debt, as well as the concept of the amortization schedule and the need to periodically reconcile the debt account.

Basic Debt Accounting

Debt is defined as an amount owed for funds borrowed. This may take a variety of forms, such as:
- Credit card debt, which can either be paid off each month or carried forward in exchange for a high interest rate.
- A line of credit, which is used to meet short-term needs, and which is usually limited to the amount of collateral that the borrower has available to guarantee repayment. A line of credit balance may fluctuate up or down during a year, and is expected to be paid off at least once a year.
- A promissory note, which is a fixed sum that a business borrows and then commits to pay back over time, in accordance with a fixed repayment schedule.

There are several issues that the borrower must be aware of when accounting for debt. The initial issue is how to classify the debt in the accounting records. Here are the main areas to be concerned with:
- If the debt is payable within one year, record the debt in a short-term debt account; this is a liability account. The typical line of credit is payable within one year, and so is classified as short-term debt.
- If the debt is payable in more than one year, record the debt in a long-term debt account; this is a liability account.
- If a loan agreement contains a clause stating that the lender can demand payment at any time, classify the debt as a current liability. This is the case

even if there is no expectation that the lender will demand payment within the current year.

- If the debt is in the form of a credit card statement, this is typically handled as an account payable, and so is simply recorded through the accounts payable module in the accounting software.

The next debt accounting issue is how to determine the amount of interest expense associated with debt. This is usually quite easy, since the lender includes the amount of the interest expense on its periodic billing statements to the company. In the case of a line of credit, the borrower is probably required to maintain its primary checking account with the lending bank, so the bank simply deducts the interest from the checking account once a month. This amount is usually identified as an interest charge on the monthly bank statement, so one can easily identify and record it as part of the monthly bank reconciliation adjustments. Alternatively, the lender may provide an amortization schedule to the borrower, which states the proportions of interest expense and loan repayment that will comprise each subsequent payment made to the lender. See the next section for a description of an amortization schedule.

As an alternative, the amount of interest expense can be calculated with the following formula:

Outstanding debt × Interest rate × Days outstanding = Interest expense

For example, the owners of a casino have taken out a $200,000 loan at an interest rate of 8%. At the end of one month, the related interest expense is:

$200,000 Debt × 8% Interest × 1/12 Year = $1,333.33

A lender may require a small commitment fee for the unused balance of a line of credit. This is essentially another form of interest expense. For example, a business negotiates for a $500,000 line of credit, and is currently using $380,000 of this amount, leaving $120,000 unused. The company's lender charges a ¼% fee on the unused balance each month, which is $300 (calculated as $120,000 unused funds × 0.0025).

Debt Accounting

The next issue is how to account for the various debt-related transactions. They are as follows:

- *Initial loan.* When a loan is first taken out, debit the cash account and credit either the short-term debt account or long-term debt account, depending on the nature of the loan. For example, a company borrows $1,000,000. The entry is:

	Debit	Credit
Cash	1,000,000	
Long-term debt		1,000,000

- *Interest payment.* If there is no immediate loan repayment, with only interest being paid, then the entry is a debit to the interest expense account and a credit to the cash account. For example, the interest rate on the $1,000,000 just described is 7%, with payments due at the end of each year. After one year, the entry is:

	Debit	Credit
Interest expense	70,000	
Cash		70,000

- *Commitment fee.* If a portion of the funds set aside by a lender for a line of credit is unused, a commitment fee may be charged to the borrower. The entry is a debit to the interest expense account and a credit to the cash account. For example, the monthly ¼% commitment fee on $100,000 of unused line of credit is $250. The entry is:

	Debit	Credit
Interest expense	250	
Cash		250

- *Mixed payment.* If a payment is being made that includes both interest expense and a loan repayment, debit the interest expense account, debit the applicable loan liability account, and credit the cash account. For example, a $5,000 loan payment is comprised of $4,300 of interest expense and $700 of loan repayment. The entry is:

	Debit	Credit
Interest expense	4,300	
Short-term debt	700	
Cash		5,000

- *Final payment.* If there is a final balloon payment where most or all of the debt is repaid, debit the applicable loan liability account and credit the cash account. For example, a company has been paying nothing but interest on a $500,000 loan for the past four years, and now repays the entire loan balance. The entry is:

	Debit	Credit
Short-term debt	500,000	
Cash		500,000

The Amortization Schedule

An amortization schedule is a table that states the periodic payments to be made as part of a loan agreement, and which notes the following information on each line of the table:

- Payment number
- Payment due date
- Payment total
- Interest component of payment
- Principal component of payment
- Ending principal balance remaining

Thus, the calculation on each line of the amortization schedule is designed to arrive at the ending principal balance for each period, for which the calculation is:

Beginning principal balance - (Payment total - Interest expense) = Ending principal balance

The amortization schedule is extremely useful for accounting for each payment in a promissory note, since it separates the interest and principal components of each payment. The schedule is also useful for modeling how the remaining loan liability will vary if you accelerate or delay payments, or alter their size. An amortization schedule can also encompass balloon payments and even negative amortization situations where the principal balance increases over time.

A sample amortization schedule follows, where a borrower has taken on a $50,000 loan that is to be repaid with five annual payments, using an interest rate of 8%. Note how the proportion of interest expense to the total payment made rapidly declines, until there is almost no interest expense remaining in the final payment. The schedule also notes the total interest expense associated with the loan.

Sample Amortization Schedule

Year	Beginning Loan Balance	Loan Payment	8% Interest	Loan Repayment	Ending Loan Balance
1	$50,000	$12,523	$4,000	$8,523	$41,477
2	41,477	12,523	3,318	9,205	32,272
3	32,272	12,523	2,582	9,941	22,331
4	22,331	12,523	1,786	10,737	11,594
5	11,594	12,522	928	11,594	0
		$62,614	$12,614	$50,000	

* Note: The Year 5 payment was reduced by $1 to offset the effects of rounding.

Reconciling the Debt Account

It is essential to periodically compare the remaining loan balance reported by the lender to the balance reported on the books of the casino. It is entirely possible that there will be a difference, for which there are usually two reasons. They are:

- The loan payments made by the borrower to the lender arrived either earlier or later than the payment due date. This alters the amount of interest expense charged to the borrower.
- The most recent loan payment made by the borrower to the lender is still in transit to the lender, or has not yet been recorded by the lender in its accounting system.

If there is a difference, contact the lender and determine the nature of the difference. If the interest charge recognized by the lender varies from the amount recognized by the borrower, alter the borrower's interest expense to match the amount recognized by the lender. If the difference is due to a payment in transit, no adjustment to the accounting records needs to be made.

The reason why this reconciliation is so necessary is that the casino's auditors will contact the lender at the end of the year to confirm with them the amount owed by the company. If the auditors discover a difference, they will require the casino to adjust its loan records.

Summary

Though debt accounting should not be especially difficult, we must emphasize the need to reconcile the debt account at regular intervals. This is an area in which the amounts of interest recognized by the lender and borrower can easily diverge, resulting in notable differences. It is better to locate and eliminate these differences prior to year-end, rather than having the auditors discover them.

Chapter 9
Controls and Policies

Introduction

Any gaming business is essentially a cash business, on a par with a banking institution. It takes in, holds, and disburses large amounts of cash, much of which is needed to fund its daily operations. Further, the cash may be located throughout the enterprise, at table games, slot machines, money changing operations, and the cage. Given the massive amount and widespread distribution of cash, casinos must implement the strongest possible cash controls to avoid losses. The applicable gaming commissions also mandate strict controls, since they have a vested interest in casinos reporting the highest possible revenue levels that can then be taxed.

In the following sections, we briefly cover several types of gaming theft, and then dive into dozens of controls that can be used to mitigate the risk of theft. In addition, we provide a sampling of the tasks that an internal audit team could pursue to detect control breaches and fraud, and finish with several accounting policies that are specific to casinos, and which can be used to set boundaries for acceptable levels of behavior.

Types of Gaming Theft

There are many ways to steal from a gaming operation, since there are large amounts of cash and cash equivalents located throughout the facility. Here are several examples:

- *Card counting.* Some experienced customers can keep track of the cards already played, in which case they can modify their betting based on the mix of cards remaining in the deck. This activity is illegal in some locations, but is permitted in other areas.
- *Collusion.* Several players can signal to each other the contents of their hands. Alternatively, the dealer can signal the players.
- *Counterfeit money.* A customer can exchange counterfeit bills for chips or credits on a slot machine, so that the casino takes the loss on the counterfeit money. The problem is exacerbated if the customer then exchanges his chips at the cage for cash, in which case the person walks out with real bills.
- *Employee theft.* Employees can tuck small amounts of bills, coins, and chips into their pockets or other locations before the items can be counted, which is anywhere from the gaming tables to the count rooms.
- *Marker conversion.* A customer signs a marker in exchange for chips, which he then exchanges for cash; the marker is never paid.
- *Misdirected fills.* A cashier could create a fill transaction to send chips out of the cage, at which point they are removed from the premises.

- *Palming*. A dealer can palm chips during the course of a game.
- *Pinching and pressing*. A customer pulls his wager off a gaming table if he can see that his bet is about to lose, which is called pinching. Conversely, he can add to his bet if he can see that his bet is about to win, which is called pressing.
- *Slot machine theft*. An employee uses a key to open a slot machine and steal coins from the hopper or drop bucket.

Later in this chapter, we describe a number of controls that can reduce the occurrence of these types of theft.

Accounting Controls

A casino should have a system of procedures and controls in place that adequately ensures that the following goals are met:
- Assets are properly safeguarded
- Assets can only be accessed with management authorization
- Financial records are reliably maintained and accurate
- There is an adequate segregation of duties
- Transactions are properly authorized by management

Doing so requires both a broad and deep set of controls that is constantly monitored.

In order to receive a gaming license from the applicable regulatory authority, a gaming establishment has to submit written documentation of a strong system of internal controls. The documentation covers every aspect of a gaming organization, including the following:
- Accounting activities
- Administrative activities
- Job descriptions for all positions
- Operating procedures for the gaming area
- Organization chart and reporting relationships
- Physical safeguards

Depending on the regulatory authority, a gaming entity may need to have its written controls documentation examined by an independent auditor. The intent of this examination is to note any instances in which the actual and documented controls diverge.

The state governments that receive tax income from casinos and other gaming operations have a vested interest in the presence of strong controls, since tax payments are lower if people are skimming revenue. Consequently, many state gaming commissions mandate the presence of a strong system of controls.

In the following section, we describe many controls that can be used to form a robust control environment.

Controls

There are several types of controls. *Procedural controls* are integrated into the processes used throughout a casino. For example, the process of moving cash and chips from a gaming table to the count room is replete with controls, such as the use of keys to remove a drop box, another key to store it on a transport trolley, and another key to open the box. An essential part of procedural controls is the separation of duties, where many people are involved in the handling, counting, and processing of cash and chips. When a number of people are involved in processes, it is much more difficult for one individual to engage in fraud.

Documentary controls are the manual or computerized tabulations of information, which are compared to other documents to look for discrepancies. When there is a complete set of documentary controls, it is possible to trace a transaction back through the various steps to its origination point, and note the most likely point along the way where a problem might have occurred.

In the following sub-sections, we list procedural and documentary controls that can be implemented throughout a casino.

Comp Controls

We begin with controls over complimentary items; these are essentially marketing expenditures that are needed to initially attract customers into a casino, and retain them once they arrive. Possible controls are:

- Use a formal hierarchy of complimentary services that matches the loss experience of a customer to the amount of comps granted.
- Require management approval of incremental comps above the comps stated in a customer's position in the comp hierarchy.
- The manual addition of points to a player's tracking account must be approved by a supervisor.
- Restrict access to the database of promotional accounts to authorized personnel, so that unauthorized comps cannot be added.
- Maintain a log of changes to the database of promotional accounts, and review the log regularly. This control may detect instances in which someone attempted to issue an unauthorized comp.
- When it is necessary to control comp expenses more closely, require more comps to be approved in advance by more senior levels of management.

Credit Controls

Next, we assume that a customer has been attracted by comps, and now applies for credit. This represents a potentially large bad debt risk for a casino, and so requires deep controls, such as:

- Use a standard procedure for deriving the amount of credit to grant to each customer, along with tiers of approvals for higher credit levels. This results in the consistent granting of credit.

- Markers are prenumbered, and there is a system in place for keeping track of them.
- Unused marker forms are stored in a locked cabinet, and forms are logged when issued. This prevents the forms from being stolen and used to obtain chips.
- There is a system in place for promptly recording markers in the casino computer system.
- Do not hand over a marker to a customer without first checking some form of valid identification. Otherwise, credit may be granted to someone not associated with the credit information that formed the basis for the amount on the marker.
- Ensure that the signature used to sign a marker is the same as the one used to sign the supporting credit application. Otherwise, a customer could claim that he never signed a marker.
- Impose an adequate level of control over the information in the credit files, so that credit levels cannot be altered without proper authorization.
- Note in each customer's credit file the name of the person who granted each increment of credit to the individual, including temporary increases.
- There is a system in place for warning the credit staff whenever there is evidence that a customer is not paying down his credit balance in a timely manner.
- Impose an adequate level of segregation of duties between the approval, issuance, and collection of credit.

Front Money

A new customer may deposit cash at the cage, which is intended to fund the person's gaming activities. The following controls may apply:
- Receipts issued to customers for their deposits should be sequentially numbered for tracking purposes and issued in two parts. The receipts should also fully document the identification of the customer and the amount deposited.
- Customers are given one copy of each completed receipt, while the other copy is retained by the cage staff. Thus, two parties have a record of the transaction.
- There is a daily reconciliation of customer deposits and withdrawals from their accounts, in order to spot record keeping anomalies.

Bingo Controls

Once customers are funded with credit or have deposited front money, they disperse to the gaming locations within the casino. One possible destination is the bingo parlor, where the following controls could be used:
- Maintain tight control over the inventory of bingo cards, beginning with their transport from the supplier, continuing through the receiving function,

and their final on-site storage. This prevents cards from being stolen and used during games.

- All bingo cards have a unique serial number by which they can be identified. This is used to spot cards that are false or which are being used in the wrong game.
- Log the beginning and ending card numbers sold for each bingo session. This sets a boundary around the range of cards being used.
- Voided bingo cards should be physically mutilated, so that they cannot be used during play.
- Bingo funds on hand are counted and reconciled to the amounts recorded in the system.
- Require that the voiding of bingo card sales stop before the calling of a game begins.
- Winning payout cards are verified to ensure that they are associated with the correct session, and that their serial numbers have not been altered.
- Verify that all 75 balls used to select numbers are present and have not been damaged.

Keno Controls

Another gaming location within a casino is the keno room, for which the following controls can be used:

- Keno balls are inspected prior to play by two people, to ensure that all numbers are accounted for and that none of the balls have been damaged.
- Keno personnel cannot access the random number generator. Otherwise, they could alter the outcome of a game.
- Keno tickets are recorded on a computer log that is not accessible by the keno staff, so that they cannot alter any betting records.
- Keno tickets cannot be written or voided once number selections have begun. Otherwise someone could buy a ticket when there is certain knowledge of the outcome.
- A supervisor must countersign all voided keno tickets, to ensure that the voiding process has been followed correctly.
- The keno number selection process is recorded by a surveillance camera system, to see if anyone has altered or interfered with the selection process.
- A supervisor from outside the keno department must approval all larger payouts, to ensure that the payouts are valid.
- Documentation must be retained for all keno payouts, in case it is necessary to investigate a game at a later date.

Race and Sports Book Controls

Controls for the race and sports book area are quite similar to those used for keno, since the betting process is approximately the same. Relevant controls are:

- All ticket information is recorded on a computer log that is not accessible by the race and sports book staff.
- Race and sports book tickets cannot be written or voided after the start of an event, for which there is a cut-off time in the system.
- Supervisors must authorize all voided tickets.
- A supervisor from outside the race and sports book department must approve all larger payouts, to ensure that the payouts are valid.
- Documentation must be retained for all pay outs.
- The ticket associated with a payout is stamped as paid, along with the payment amount and date paid, so that the ticket cannot be presented again.

Slot Machine Controls

Slot machines contain cash that could theoretically be accessed, and they are located within reach of customers, which presents an opportunity for theft. Consequently, there are a large number of controls in this area, including the following:

- Require an examination of video footage of the face of a slot machine for which a jackpot has been awarded, to verify that the amount paid matches the information on the machine.
- If the payout from a slot machine is quite large, schedule it for a mandatory maintenance check, to ensure that it is functioning properly.
- All slot jackpots exceeding a threshold amount must be approved by a supervisor before they can be paid out, to ensure that the amount paid is correct.
- A customer must provide identification for a larger jackpot, so that a Form W-2G can be filled out.
- Keep the amount of coins in the slot hopper relatively low, so that a cheater cannot illegally access the hopper and cause a substantial loss. This means that the winners of jackpots must instead be paid from the cage or coin booth. However, this increases the labor cost of issuing jackpot payments. Also, a manual payout takes longer, and is an inconvenience to customers. Consequently, the hopper load can be reduced *too* far.
- Maintain a machine access log inside each slot machine, noting who has opened a slot machine, when it happened, and why. This information can be used to trace who might be incorrectly altering a machine or removing bills or coins from it.
- Record all meter readings in ink, so that they cannot be subsequently altered to match a reduced number of coins (the rest having been stolen).
- Maintain a log of the frequency of jackpot payouts, both by machine and time period, to see if there has been an unusual level of frequency that could indicate tampering with certain slot machines.

- Require a security person to be present when a maintenance technician opens a slot machine that is a progressive slot machine, contains an unusually large hopper, or has a large jackpot size. Doing so reduces the risk of theft, or of manipulating a machine that has a large payoff.
- Have a procedure for removing all coins from a slot machine that is being sent to the maintenance shop, including bagging and counting the coins and transferring them to the cage for safekeeping.
- Lock down access to the slot machine repair area, so that an unauthorized person cannot gain access and tamper with machines that are under repair.
- Link all slot machines to a central management system, which is notified whenever a machine is opened. This can trigger an investigation, or at least video surveillance to monitor what is being done to a machine.

Dealer Controls

There are a multitude of opportunities for theft in the gaming table area, since a number of people are handling chips that are convertible into cash. The following controls provide a sample of the full range of control opportunities.

- Track the table assignments of all dealers and the times when they are on duty. Then trace table losses back to the dealers assigned to those tables. If there is a consistent pattern of losses associated with a specific dealer, the dealer may be engaged in cheating.
- If the preceding control indicates that a dealer may be cheating, ask the surveillance team to closely monitor this dealer.
- When a dealer leaves a table or moves chips to or from the chip rack, he must turn his hands upward with fingers fully extended, which is called clearing hands. The intent is to keep the dealer from palming and making off with chips.
- Dealers are trained in body position, so that they have a full view of the table while dealing cards. They are also instructed to maintain a watch over their table even while conversing with a supervisor, who may be standing off to one side or behind the dealer.
- Dealers must indicate which chips have been given to them as gratuities by players, so that the denominations of the chips can be viewed by surveillance cameras.
- Dealers must maintain a highly organized chip rack, with denominations clearly segregated, so that accurate counts can be maintained.
- Dealers must wear aprons, or pants without pockets, so that they cannot slip chips into their pockets.

In general, dealers should follow procedures as closely as possible, so that their movements follow a consistent pattern. If there is a break in their movements that varies from procedure, this can trigger a suspicion that they are engaging in illegal activities, which calls for closer investigation.

It is possible that losses linked to a specific dealer are not the fault of the dealer. If the dealer is inexperienced, card counters may prefer to sit at this dealer's table, where their activities are less likely to be noticed.

Chip and Token Controls

The main issue with chips and tokens is that they are a substitute for cash within a casino, and so must be protected in the same manner as cash. If chips or tokens are stolen at any point in the supply chain or within a casino, someone can then present them to a cashier for conversion into cash. The following controls can help to maintain control over them:

- Buy chips and tokens from reputable suppliers that maintain tight control over their inventories. Otherwise, chips could be stolen at the supplier and then presented at the cage for payment.
- Require suppliers to only accept chip and token orders from authorized buyers within the company. Otherwise, an outsider could place an order and take delivery of a substantial number of chips.
- Inspect all received packages of chips and tokens to see if any have been removed. Again, stolen chips could then be converted into cash at the cage.
- Inspect all received packages of chips and tokens to verify that the received amounts and denominations match the amounts requested on the purchase order.
- Store excess chips and tokens in the vault, to reduce the risk of theft.
- When chips or tokens are to be destroyed, have a specialist chip destruction firm come to the casino and destroy them under the oversight of the security staff.

Table Game Controls

There are several additional controls associated with table games that involve the handling of chips and paperwork. These controls are:

- If a table is not currently in use, the chips associated with it are stored in a secure location.
- Alternatively, if a table is being shut down for just a short period of time, the chips are secured under a locking cover.
- Schedule a periodic review of cards and dice that are no longer being used to see if they have been marked or altered in any way.
- Deface or destroy old, used cards and dice so that they cannot be used again at the gaming tables.
- Match all fill slip copies retained by the cashier to the other copies of these slips that are deposited in the table drop boxes. This ensures that pay outs by the cage staff are actually going to the tables.

Ticket Controls

If a TITO system is used to bypass the need for coins in slot machines, then the resulting tickets can be a source of fraud. The following controls can mitigate this risk:

- Buy paper stock for the tickets that contains a watermark, so that it is difficult for a forger to duplicate.
- Lock up the paper stock used to print tickets from the slot machines, so that the paper cannot be stolen and used to print fake tickets.
- Maintain control over the number of tickets issued to each slot machine, so that excess tickets are not "lost."
- Shred all paper stock that will not be used, so that no one can obtain the excess stock and use it to create false tickets.
- Include the machine number, date, time, and amount of the pay out on each ticket, as well as a unique identification number. This level of specificity allows one to trace a jackpot back to a machine and the associated surveillance video recordings.
- The cashier should notify a supervisor if a ticket is presented that states an amount different from what is stated in the casino database for the same identification number. This control is needed to identify customers who have fraudulently altered the payment amounts on their tickets.

Collection Controls

If customers leave a casino without paying off their markers, additional controls are needed to reduce the risk of loss from bad debts. Possible controls are:

- Compare markers to the accounts receivable aging to ensure that all markers are present and correctly recorded.
- Require formal approval by management of marker write-offs or write-downs. The authorized person should not be responsible for the initial issuance of credit.

Key Access Controls

A central part of the process of moving currency, chips and tokens from the casino floor to the count rooms is the use of keys to lock down assets. The relevant controls are:

- Two keys should be required for all drop boxes; one to release it from its principal location, and another to open it.
- Keys are only issued to someone listed on an approved key access list.
- No one is allowed access to both sets of keys – that is, they can either remove a drop box from a location *or* they can open it, but not both. In more detail:
  o The drop box release key is controlled by the security staff.
  o The drop box contents key is controlled by the cage, and is used by the count team.

- A key access log is maintained that notes which keys were issued, to whom, and the dates and times when the keys were issued and returned. The log can include the signatures of all parties issuing and receiving keys.
- Keys and locks are only ordered from a supplier that specializes in high-security keys and locks.

In addition to the two keys just described, there is also a double lock on the count room door, which requires keys from both security and the count team to gain access. Further, the trolley used to transport drop boxes, drop buckets, and currency acceptor containers from their pickup points to the count rooms is also locked, using two locks. Access to one lock is controlled by security, while the other is controlled by the cage.

Count Team Controls

We now move to controls over count teams, which are used to count the currency collected from the casino floor. Applicable controls are:

- The owners and senior managers of a casino are not allowed in the count rooms, since their higher level of authority could allow them to override controls.
- The count team members cannot be from the casino floor staff, since this is not an adequate separation of duties.
- Counts must be scheduled within specific time blocks, in case regulators want to send observers.
- The credentials of each member of the drop box count team are examined by a security guard before they are allowed into the count room to count drop boxes. A double lock is used, so that the security staff must also unlock the count room door.
- The count team members wear smocks or jumpsuits that contain no pockets, so that they cannot illicitly hide chips or currency in their clothes.
- The contents of each drop box are unloaded onto a table that has video surveillance. One team member empties the drop boxes, while another member sorts the contents and conducts an initial count. A third member recounts the box contents and fills out a summary form. This separates the count duties.
- The table on which counts are tabulated is made of clear Plexiglas, so that any currency falling under the table is immediately obvious.
- Have a security officer present in the count room during all counts, which can be a deterrent to the theft of funds by count team members.
- When a hard count is being conducted, the scale used to weigh the contents of a drop bucket is calibrated, to ensure that it does not generate variances between the amounts counted and weighed.
- When anyone on a count team leaves the count room, they must first pass through a metal detector to see if they have illicitly brought out any coins or tokens.

- The count team signs the count sheets resulting from the counting process, to take responsibility for the count.

Physical Access Controls

It is critical to maintain strong controls over all access to currency and chip storage areas. For example:
- Install a man trap in front of the vault and count rooms. This is a segregated room that requires key access to enter and exit before entering the vault or a count room. The exit door cannot be opened until the entrance door is closed. A man trap makes it more difficult for someone to gain access to a secure area, and also allows security to lock both doors while someone is in the man trap.
- Physically separate the count areas from the vault, so that no one on a count team has direct access to primary currency and chip storage.
- Lock up the empty drop boxes, so that no one can adjust them to be accessed while they are in use at the gaming tables.

Vault Controls

The main control over the vault area is (obviously) to have an extremely secure vault, as noted in the preceding set of physical access controls. In addition, the following controls can be applied:
- Install comprehensive surveillance camera coverage of the vault.
- Have unannounced counts of the currency, coins and tokens stored in the vault.
- Only allow employees into the vault who are not associated with the people working in other parts of the casino.
- Prohibit the entry of senior management, or at least only allow them under tightly controlled circumstances.

Supervisor Controls

An essential control is to have supervisory oversight of all activities on the casino floor and in the cage. A supervisor can monitor the staff to ensure that procedures are properly followed, and to approve larger pay outs.

Surveillance Controls

One of the best general controls over all casino operations is a video surveillance system that blankets all activities. This is especially useful as an after-the-fact examination tool. Controls are:
- Install moveable camera systems throughout the casino floor and cage, so that the surveillance staff can monitor activities.
- Record all surveillance video on hard drives, so that the footage can be accessed later for investigatory purposes.

Form Controls

A central part of documentary controls is to maintain tight control over the forms used throughout a casino. Improper use of some forms can lead to major control breaches that can lead to the loss of funds. Sample controls are:

- Forms used in casino operations are to be stored in a locked cabinet. Examples of these forms are markers, fill slips, credit slips, and hopper fill slips.
- Forms used in casino operations are to be consecutively numbered, so that missing forms can be identified by gaps in the numbering.
- When forms are used, the form numbers used are logged. The log is used to more easily identify missing forms.
- When forms are voided, mark "Void" on them and retain the slip for reconciliation purposes, so that the forms cannot be misused.
- Use duplicate forms to document the transfer of currency and chips. The issuing and receiving parties agree on the amount being transferred and sign the forms. Each party retains one of the forms. If there is a discrepancy between the two forms, it could indicate that one of the parties altered their version, possibly to hide a theft of funds.

Information Technology Controls

Someone gaining illicit access to the computer systems of a casino could steal inordinately large sums, so controls over information technology should be especially robust. For example:

- Gaming computers are stored in a secure area, with limited access.
- Password and biometric controls are used for computer system access.
- Passwords are changed regularly.
- User accounts are locked out after a predetermined number of failed login attempts.
- Computer files are backed up continually and the backups are stored in a secure area.
- Terminated employees are immediately locked out of the system.
- Accounts established for new employees are logged and reviewed by management.
- Remote access to computer systems is strictly limited and logged.

Money Laundering Controls

An ancillary function is for a casino to issue currency transaction reports (CTRs) and suspicious activity reports (SARs) to the government when larger cash transactions are spotted. Possible controls in this area are:

- *Training.* Provide a training program and refresher classes to employees in regard to CTR requirements, and the activities that may be considered reportable SAR events.

- *Payment restrictions.* Do not issue a check or wire payment for winnings to a third party. Instead, the payment must be made to the winning customer, which means that a record now exists of the recipient of cash.
- *Require identification.* For larger cash out transactions, require a customer to provide a valid form of identification.
- *Barred from play.* If a customer involved in a large cash transaction refuses to provide a valid form of identification, that person is barred from all gaming activities until the identification is provided. This means that a barred customer database must be maintained and regularly reviewed by the staff.
- *Logging.* Maintain a multiple transaction log, in which is noted all cash transactions exceeding a certain minimum threshold. When the recorded information is aggregated, it may uncover cumulative currency transactions that require reporting on a CTR.

Internal Audit

An internal audit team is an essential component of the activities of a gaming operation, given the large amounts of cash involved and the corresponding risk of loss. The following areas are prime targets for ongoing control reviews and examinations:

Procedural Reviews

- Card game operation
- Credit determination
- Fills
- Foreign exchange conversions
- Hard counts
- Keno ticket voiding
- Key control
- Manual slot payouts
- Race and sports book
- Race and sports ticket voiding
- Slot machine access
- Soft counts
- Surveillance
- Testing the weigh scale
- Wire transfers

Reconciliations

- Comparison of bill totals removed from currency acceptors to currency acceptor bill meters on a slot machine
- Comparison of the net amount of hard count to the net coin-in and coin-out meters on a slot machine

- Comparison of drop box contents to summary report
- Comparison of gross revenue to taxable revenue
- Comparison of on-hand bills to recorded balance
- Comparison of on-hand coins to recorded balance

Reviews

- Review of receivables write-off documentation
- Review of cashier over/short balances at end of shift
- Review of large winning race and sports tickets, including examination of the point spread and when tickets were purchased versus the event start time
- Review of all unpaid winners and verification that a corresponding liability has been recorded
- Review of form usage logs to see if any forms have been incorrectly removed from storage

The internal audit team cannot report to the operational management group of a casino, since there is a risk that the management group can influence the findings of the audit team. Instead, this group reports to the audit committee or board of directors.

Indicators of Control Weaknesses

A test of the robustness of a system of controls at an aggregate level is the hold percentage. *Hold* is the amount of money that a casino retains after betting ceases. The *hold percentage* is the relationship between the amount that was bet and lost by customers, in aggregate. For example, if the house advantage on a game is 4%, then the hold percentage on that game for $100 of betting should be:

Drop	$100
Paid out	96
Hold	4
Hold percentage	4%

The percentage calculated in the preceding table is the theoretical hold percentage. The actual hold percentage should be quite close to this number, especially after a large number of games have been played. If not, and there is instead a notable fluctuation in the hold percentage, this indicates that there may be a problem that could generate losses for the casino. The following could all be investigated if there is a hold percentage variance:

- *Play volume*. If there was unusually low game volume during the measurement period, the actual hold percentage could vary from the theoretical percentage. An unusual losing or winning streak by a few players could cause a variance.

- *High rollers.* If a single high roller has a win streak while betting large amounts, the casino could suffer a substantial short-term loss.
- *Equipment maintenance.* The gaming equipment could have malfunctioned. This can mean checking the performance of the slot machines, keno equipment, and roulette wheels.
- *Cheating.* When all other options have been investigated, the default presumption is that someone has engaged in cheating to win, or has engaged in theft to steal funds.

Policies

A casino should have several policies that govern the financial aspects of its operations. These policies are intended to set boundaries around the limits of acceptable activities, so that losses can be contained. Several policies follow.

Credit Policy

A key policy is the credit authorization policy. An ill-considered extension of credit could lead to a significant loss, so an increasing number of approvals should be required for larger amounts of credit, as noted in the following example.

Credit Authorization Table

	Required Authorizers
Temporary Credit	
Up to $10,000	Credit Manager
$10,001 to $50,000	Credit Manager | CFO
$50,001 to $100,000	Credit Manager | CFO | President
Permanent Credit	
Up to $50,000	Credit Manager | CFO
$50,001 to $100,000	Credit Manager | CFO | President
$100,000 +	Credit Committee

Credit Write-Off Policy

A casino may elect to write off a portion of the amount owed by a customer, in exchange for being paid a reduced amount. The amount of this write-off can be substantial, so it is imperative that a sufficiently senior-level person authorize it. The write-off authorization level can track the authorizer list noted in the preceding credit authorization table, using different threshold levels as appropriate.

Fixed Asset Disposal Policy

Government regulations can limit the number of entities to which used slot machines can be sold, on the grounds that the buyer must have a gaming license. Accordingly, consider a policy that mandates sales of used equipment only to properly licensed buyers.

Jackpot Approval Policy

It may be useful to have a jackpot approval policy, where smaller jackpots are paid on the spot, but larger ones require the approval of at least the slot manager and security manager. These individuals may need to examine the slot machine in question and any security videos to see if tampering caused a jackpot to be paid.

Winnings Claim Period Policy

Management may set a time limit during which winnings can be claimed, such as within 90 days. This period may be set by the governing gaming commission. Doing so allows for the elimination of liabilities related to winnings that might otherwise extend for an indeterminate period of time.

Ticket Payout Redemption Period

As was the case with the winnings claim period policy, management can set a time limit policy for the period during which TITO tickets can be redeemed, such as one month. Doing so keeps a casino from piling up a large long-term liability for unredeemed tickets that may never be presented.

Summary

The controls used by a gaming operation are absolutely critical to its ability to obtain a gaming license, as well as to avoid losses due to the theft of currency, chips, and tokens. The controls noted in this chapter provide a reasonable basis for an adequate system of controls. However, the licensing gaming authorities may very well have more comprehensive systems of controls that they require a gaming entity to have in place. Also, a controls consultant can examine a casino's specific systems and spot areas in which additional controls are warranted. Consequently, treat the controls list in this chapter as merely a basic framework around which additional controls can be layered.

Chapter 10
Financial Reports

Introduction

The financial statements are comprised of the income statement, balance sheet, and statement of cash flows. The income statement contains the results of its operations during a reporting period, showing revenues and expenses, and the resulting profit or loss. The balance sheet summarizes the assets, liabilities, and equity of a casino as of a specific point in time. Finally, the statement of cash flows summarizes all cash inflow and outflows experienced during a reporting period. We address the layout of these statements in the following sections, along with a brief discussion of alternative forms of reporting.

Calculation of Income Statement

The income statement that a casino reports to the outside world matches the standard format used in other industries, where expense line items are deducted from revenues to arrive at a profit or loss figure. However, this terminology differs *within* a casino. A table showing the differences in terminology follows.

Comparison of Income Statement Terminology

Standard Income Statement	=	Internal Casino Terminology
Gross revenue	=	Drop
Cost of goods sold	=	Paid outs
Gross profit	=	Net revenue
Operating expenses	=	Operating expenses
Profit	=	Profit

The internal casino terminology only appears in the accounting records, not in the financial statements.

The Income Statement

The income statement is designed to reveal the results of the operations and financing activities of a business during a reporting period. It begins with revenues and subtracts out expenses to arrive at a gain or loss.

The Securities and Exchange Commission (SEC) has issued guidance regarding how expenses are to be presented on the income statement by entities that have combined casino-hotel operations. The SEC staff believes that the expenses

157

associated with each of the revenue-producing activities (i.e., casino, hotel, and restaurant operations) be separately presented in the income statement. By doing so, a reader of the income statement can discern operating profit levels for each individual revenue-producing activity. This layout appears in the following sample income statement, where revenue and expenses are divided into each revenue-producing activity.

Sample Casino Income Statement

Revenue	
Gaming	$1,000,000
Rooms	250,000
Food and beverage	50,000
Other	10,000
	$1,310,000
Less: Promotional allowances	-60,000
Net revenues	1,250,000
Expenses	
Gaming	400,000
Rooms	125,000
Food and beverage	25,000
Other	2,000
Selling, general and administrative	500,000
Depreciation and amortization	80,000
Total operating costs and expenses	1,132,000
Operating income	118,000
Interest expense	-18,000
Income before income taxes	100,000
Less: Provision for income taxes	35,000
Net income	$65,000

The Balance Sheet

A balance sheet (also known as a statement of financial position) presents information about an entity's assets, liabilities, and shareholders' equity, where the compiled result must match this formula:

$$\text{Total assets} = \text{Total liabilities} + \text{Equity}$$

The balance sheet reports the aggregate effect of transactions as of a specific date. The balance sheet is used to assess an entity's liquidity and ability to pay its debts.

There is no specific requirement for the line items to be included in the balance sheet. The following line items, at a minimum, are normally included in it:

Current Assets:

- Cash and cash equivalents
- Receivables
- Investments
- Inventories

Non-Current Assets:

- Property, plant, and equipment
- Intangible assets
- Goodwill

Current Liabilities:

- Trade and other payables
- Accrued expenses
- Current tax liabilities
- Current portion of loans payable
- Other financial liabilities
- Liabilities held for sale

Non-Current Liabilities:

- Loans payable
- Deferred tax liabilities
- Other non-current liabilities

Equity:

- Capital stock
- Additional paid-in capital
- Retained earnings

Here is an example of a balance sheet which presents information as of the end of two fiscal years:

Pirates Casino
Balance Sheet
As of December 31, 20X2 and 20X1

(000s)	12/31/20X2	12/31/20x1
ASSETS		
Current assets		
Cash and cash equivalents	$270,000	$215,000
Trade receivables	147,000	139,000
Inventories – food and beverage	139,000	128,000
Other current assets	15,000	27,000
Total current assets	$571,000	$509,000
Non-current assets		
Property, plant, and equipment	551,000	529,000
Goodwill	82,000	82,000
Other intangible assets	143,000	143,000
Total non-current assets	$776,000	$754,000
Total assets	$1,347,000	$1,263,000
LIABILITIES AND EQUITY		
Current liabilities		
Trade and other payables	$217,000	$198,000
Short-term borrowings	133,000	202,000
Current portion of long-term borrowings	5,000	5,000
Current tax payable	26,000	23,000
Accrued expenses	9,000	13,000
Total current liabilities	$390,000	$441,000
Non-current liabilities		
Long-term debt	85,000	65,000
Deferred taxes	19,000	17,000
Total non-current liabilities	$104,000	$82,000
Total liabilities	$494,000	$523,000
Shareholders' equity		
Capital	100,000	100,000
Additional paid-in capital	15,000	15,000
Retained earnings	738,000	625,000
Total equity	$853,000	$740,000
Total liabilities and equity	$1,347,000	$1,263,000

The Statement of Cash Flows

The statement of cash flows contains information about the flows of cash into and out of a company; in particular, it shows the extent of those company activities that generate and use cash and cash equivalents. It is particularly useful for assessing the differences between net income and the related cash receipts and payments.

> **Note:** A cash equivalent (for the purposes of the statement of cash flows) is a highly liquid investment having a maturity of three months or less. It should be at minimal risk of a change in value. Examples of cash equivalents are marketable securities, money market funds, and short-term government bonds. To be classified as a cash equivalent, an item must be unrestricted, so that it is available for immediate use.

The statement of cash flows does not replace the income statement. The income statement measures the revenues, expenses, and profit or loss generated during a reporting period. The cash flows that appear on the statement of cash flows do not necessarily match the income and loss information on the income statement, so both statements are needed to provide the most complete picture of the results generated by an entity.

Statement Requirements

The following general requirements apply to the statement of cash flows:
- *Cash balance matching.* The beginning and ending amounts of cash and cash equivalents shown in the statement of cash flows should match the amounts of cash and cash equivalents shown in the balance sheet for the same dates.
- *Reconciliation.* There shall be a reconciliation of the net income of a business to its net cash flow from operating activities, which shall report all major classes of reconciling items in separate line items. If the direct method is used (see the next section), the reconciliation shall be provided in a separate schedule. If the indirect method is used (see the Indirect Method section), the reconciliation can be integrated into the statement of cash flows, or provided as a separate schedule.
- *Gross reporting.* Cash inflows related to a financing or investing event should be separately reported from cash outflows. For example, the amounts spent to acquire fixed assets should be stated separately from the amounts received from the sale of fixed assets.

EXAMPLE

Executive Casino sells a helicopter and uses the proceeds to buy another helicopter. The proceeds from the sale of the old helicopter should be presented separately from the funds used to buy the replacement.

Junket Casino issues bonds, and uses the proceeds to pay off an existing debt obligation. The proceeds from the bond issuance should be reported separately from the funds used to pay off the old debt.

Reporting Classifications

In the statement of cash flows, cash flow information is to be reported within three separate classifications. The use of classifications is intended to improve the quality of the information presented. These classifications are:

- *Operating activities.* These are an entity's primary revenue-producing activities. Operating activities is the default classification, so if a cash flow does not belong in either of the following two classifications, it belongs in this classification. Operating cash flows are generally associated with revenues and expenses. Examples of cash inflows from operating activities are cash receipts from casino win, the sale of goods or services, accounts receivable, lawsuit settlements, normal insurance settlements, and supplier refunds. Examples of cash outflows for operating activities are for payments to employees and suppliers, fees and fines, lawsuit settlements, cash payments to lenders for interest, contributions to charity, and cash refunds to customers. Sample operating activities are segregated into cash inflows and outflows in the following table.

Sample Operating Activity Cash Inflows and Outflows

Cash Inflows	Cash Outflows
Cash receipts from the sale of goods and services	Cash payments to employees
Cash receipts from the collection of receivables	Cash payments to suppliers
Cash receipts from lawsuit settlements	Cash payment of fines
Cash receipts from settlement of insurance claims	Cash payments to settle lawsuits
Cash receipts from supplier refunds	Cash payments of taxes
Cash receipts from licensees	Cash refunds to customers
	Cash payments to settle asset retirement obligations
	Cash payment of interest to creditors
	Cash payment of contributions

- *Investing activities.* These are investments in productive assets, as well as in the debt and equity securities issued by other entities. These cash flows are generally associated with the purchase or sale of assets. Examples are cash receipts from the sale or collection of loans, the sale of securities issued by other entities, the sale of long-term assets, and the proceeds from insurance settlements related to damaged property. Examples of cash outflows from investing activities are cash payments for loans made to other entities, the purchase of the debt or equity of other entities, and the purchase of fixed assets (including capitalized interest). Sample investing activities are segregated into cash inflows and outflows in the following table.

Sample Investing Activity Cash Inflows and Outflows

Cash Inflows	Cash Outflows
Cash receipts from the sale of equity investments	Cash payments made to acquire equity investments
Cash receipts from the collection of principal on a loan	Cash payments made to acquire debt securities
Cash receipts from the sale of fixed assets	Cash payments made to acquire fixed assets

- *Financing activities.* These are the activities resulting in alterations to the amount of contributed equity and an entity's borrowings. These cash flows are generally associated with liabilities or equity, and involve transactions between the reporting entity and its providers of capital. Examples are cash receipts from the sale of an entity's own equity instruments or from issuing debt, and proceeds from derivative instruments. Examples of cash outflows from financing activities are cash outlays for dividends, share repurchases, payments for debt issuance costs, and the pay down of outstanding debt. Sample financing activities are segregated into cash inflows and outflows in the following table.

Sample Financing Activity Cash Inflows and Outflows

Cash Inflows	Cash Outflows
Cash receipts from the sale of company shares	Cash payments to pay dividends
Cash receipts from the issuance of debt instruments	Cash payments to buy back company shares
Cash receipts from a mortgage	Cash payments for debt issuance costs
Cash receipts from derivative instruments	Cash payments to pay down principal on debt

The order of presentation in the statement of cash flows is as just described – operating activities, followed by investing activities, and then financing activities.

Some types of cash flows could be classified as being in more than one of the preceding classifications. If so, the designated classification should be based on the activity most likely to provide the majority of cash flows for an item.

EXAMPLE

Killer Slots has a rent-to-purchase feature on its line of slot machines, where customers can initially rent the equipment and then apply the rental payments to an outright purchase. The rental of equipment could be considered an investing activity. However, since the company earns the bulk of its cash flow from the sale of equipment, the cash flows are placed within the operating activities classification.

The *direct method* or the *indirect method* can be used to present the statement of cash flows. The direct method shows cash inflows and outflows in the operating section. The indirect method derives operating cash flows by modifying the net income figure. No matter which method is used, the total amount of cash provided or used by operations is the same. These methods are described in the following sections.

The Direct Method

The direct method of presenting the statement of cash flows presents the specific cash flows associated with items that affect cash flow. Items that typically do so include:

- Cash collected from customers
- Interest and dividends received
- Cash paid to employees
- Cash paid to suppliers
- Interest paid
- Income taxes paid

Though additional disclosures can be made, entities tend to limit their reporting to the preceding line items. The format of the direct method appears in the following example. Also included in the example is a reconciliation of net income to cash from operating activities, which is required when the direct method is used.

EXAMPLE

Arbitrary Luck Casino constructs the following statement of cash flows using the direct method:

Arbitrary Luck Casino
Statement of Cash Flows
For the year ended 12/31/20X1

Cash flows from operating activities		
Win from gaming operations	$16,000,000	
Cash paid to employees	-11,200,000	
Cash generated from operations	4,800,000	
Interest paid	-310,000	
Income taxes paid	-1,700,000	
Net cash from operating activities		$2,790,000
Cash flows from investing activities		
Purchase of fixed assets	-580,000	
Proceeds from sale of equipment	110,000	
Net cash used in investing activities		-470,000
Cash flows from financing activities		
Proceeds from issuance of common stock	1,000,000	
Proceeds from issuance of long-term debt	500,000	
Principal payments under capital lease obligation	-10,000	
Dividends paid	-450,000	
Net cash used in financing activities		1,040,000
Net increase in cash and cash equivalents		3,360,000
Cash and cash equivalents at beginning of period		1,640,000
Cash and cash equivalents at end of period		$5,000,000

Reconciliation of net income to net cash provided by operating activities:

Net income		$2,665,000
Adjustments to reconcile net income to net cash provided by operating activities:		
Depreciation and amortization	$125,000	
Provision for losses on accounts receivable	15,000	
Gain on sale of equipment	-155,000	
Increase in interest and income taxes payable	32,000	
Increase in deferred taxes	90,000	
Increase in other liabilities	18,000	
Total adjustments		125,000
Net cash provided by operating activities		$2,790,000

The standard-setting bodies encourage the use of the direct method, but it is rarely used, for the excellent reason that the information in it is difficult to assemble; companies simply do not collect and store information in the manner required for this format. Instead, they use the indirect method, which is described in the following section.

The Indirect Method

Under the indirect method of presenting the statement of cash flows, the presentation begins with net income or loss, with subsequent additions to or deductions from that amount for non-cash revenue and expense items, resulting in cash provided by operating activities. Adjustments to the net income figure that are needed to derive cash flows from operating activities include:

- Accrued revenue
- Accrued expenses, such as a provision for bad debt losses
- Noncash expenses, such as depreciation, amortization, and depletion
- Gains and losses from the sale of assets
- Change in accounts receivable
- Change in inventory
- Change in accounts payable

The format of the indirect method appears in the following example. Note that the indirect method does not include cash inflows and outflows in the cash flows from operating activities section, but rather a derivation of cash flows based on adjustments to net income.

EXAMPLE

Chipper Casino constructs the following statement of cash flows using the indirect method:

Chipper Casino
Statement of Cash Flows
For the year ended 12/31/20X3

Cash flows from operating activities		
Net income		$3,000,000
Adjustments for:		
Depreciation and amortization	$125,000	
Provision for losses on accounts receivable	20,000	
Gain on sale of facility	-65,000	
		80,000
Increase in trade receivables	-250,000	
Decrease in inventories	325,000	
Decrease in trade payables	-50,000	
		25,000
Cash generated from operations		3,105,000
Cash flows from investing activities		
Purchase of fixed assets	-500,000	
Proceeds from sale of equipment	35,000	
Net cash used in investing activities		-465,000
Cash flows from financing activities		
Proceeds from issuance of common stock	150,000	
Proceeds from issuance of long-term debt	175,000	
Dividends paid	-45,000	
Net cash used in financing activities		280,000
Net increase in cash and cash equivalents		2,920,000
Cash and cash equivalents at beginning of period		2,080,000
Cash and cash equivalents at end of period		$5,000,000

When the indirect method is used, the reporting entity should separately disclose the amounts of interest paid and income taxes paid during the period.

The key difference between the direct and indirect methods is the derivation of the cash flows from operating activities section, where the direct method requires the reporting of specific operating activity cash inflows and outflows, while the indirect method backs into this information.

When considering which presentation method to use, consider that the indirect method provides some information that does not relate to cash flows, such as depreciation and loss provisions. The presence of non-cash items in an ostensibly cash-focused report can be confusing to some readers. In addition, a large number of reconciling items can make it difficult to understand the presented information.

The indirect method is very popular, because the information required for it is relatively easily assembled from the accounts that a business normally maintains.

Financial Statement Disclosures

Financial statement disclosures are explanatory and supplemental notes that accompany the financial statements issued by a business. The exact nature of these footnotes varies, depending upon the framework used to construct the financial statements (such as GAAP or IFRS). Financial statement disclosures are an integral part of the financial statements, so you must issue them under some circumstances to users along with the financial statements.

There are an enormous number of detailed disclosures that may be required, depending upon the types of business transactions that a company engages in. Examples of topics that can be discussed by a casino are:

- The nature of operations
- The nature of promotional allowances
- How revenue is recognized
- How liabilities and revenues are calculated
- Whether breakage is considered in these calculations

A series of sample disclosures follow, which are adapted from actual public filings.

SAMPLE DISCLOSURE – NATURE OF OPERATIONS

The Company owns and operates 10 casinos in the United States, consisting of land-based and riverboat or dockside casinos. The major source of Company revenues is derived from its gaming operations. The Company is subject to the regulations of the applicable state gaming commissions, and is taxed by the states in which it operates. The Company is also subject to certain federal reporting requirements.

SAMPLE DISCLOSURE – SIGNIFICANT ACCOUNTING POLICIES

Accounts Receivable. The Company issues credit to approved casino customers following background checks and investigations of creditworthiness. Business or economic conditions or other significant events could affect the collectability of these receivables. Accounts receivable are typically non-interest bearing and are initially recorded at cost. Marker play represents a significant portion of our overall table games volume. We maintain strict controls over the issuance of markers and aggressively pursue collection from those customers who fail to pay their marker balances timely. These collection efforts are similar to those used by most large corporations when dealing with overdue customer accounts, including the mailing of statements and delinquency notices, personal contacts, the use of outside collection agencies and civil litigation. Markers are generally legally enforceable instruments in the United States. Markers are not legally enforceable instruments in some foreign countries, but the United States' assets of foreign customers may be reached to satisfy judgments entered in the United States. We consider the likelihood and difficulty of enforceability, among other factors, when we issue credit to customers who are not residents of the United States. Accounts are written off when management deems the account to be uncollectible. Recoveries of accounts previously written off are recorded when received. We reserve an estimated amount for gaming receivables that may not be collected to reduce the Company's receivables to their net carrying amount. Methodologies for estimating the allowance for doubtful accounts range from specific reserves to various percentages applied to aged receivables. Historical collection rates are considered, as are customer relationships, in determining specific reserves.

Advertising. The Company expenses the production costs of advertising the first time the advertising takes place.

Gaming promoters. A significant portion of the Company's gaming volume is generated through the use of gaming promoters, also known as junket operators. These operators introduce high-end gaming players to the casino, assist these customers with travel arrangements, and extend gaming credit to these players. In exchange for the gaming promoters' services, the Company pays the gaming promoters through commissions or revenue-sharing arrangements. The estimated portion of the gaming promoter payments that represent amounts passed through to customers is recorded net against casino revenue, and the estimated portion retained by the gaming promoter for its compensation is recorded to casino expense.

Promotional Allowances. The retail value of accommodations, food and beverage, and other services furnished to guests without charge is included in gross revenues and then deducted as casino promotional allowances. The estimated cost of providing such casino promotional allowances is included in casino expenses.

SAMPLE DISCLOSURES - REVENUE

(1) Casino revenues are measured by the aggregate net difference between gaming wins and losses, with liabilities recognized for funds deposited by customers before gaming play occurs and for chips in customers' possession. Food and beverage, rooms, and other operating revenues are recognized when services are performed. Advance deposits on rooms and advance ticket sales are recorded as customer deposits until services are provided to the customer. Sales taxes and other taxes collected from customers on behalf of governmental authorities are accounted for on a net basis and are not included in net revenues or operating expenses. The retail value of accommodations, food and beverage, and other services furnished to guests without charge is included in gross revenues and then deducted as promotional allowances.

(2) Hotel accommodations, food, and beverages furnished to customers without charge are included in gross revenue at retail value and are then deducted as promotional allowances to

arrive at net operating revenue. The Company issues coupons to customers for the purpose of generating future revenue. The value of redeemed coupons is applied against the revenue generated on the day of coupon redemption. The estimated cost of all promotional allowances is included in casino expenses. For the years ended 20X2 and 20X1, the cost of providing promotional allowances was as follows:

(000s)	20X2	20X1
Hotel rooms	$42	$39
Food and beverages	117	102
	$159	$141

Members of the Company's player clubs earn points based on their volume of play. Members can accumulate points over time, which they can redeem under the terms of the program. Points can be redeemed for cash, meals, and hotel stays. The value of the points is offset against the revenue in the period in which the points were earned.

SAMPLE DISCLOSURE – FIXED ASSETS

The Company has significant capital invested in its long-lived assets, and judgments are made in determining their estimated useful lives and salvage values and if or when an asset (or asset group) has been impaired. The accuracy of these estimates affects the amount of depreciation and amortization expense recognized in the Company's financial results and whether we have a gain or loss on the disposal of an asset. Lives are assigned to assets based on the standard policy, which is established by management as representative of the useful life of each category of asset.

We review the carrying value of long-lived assets whenever events and circumstances indicate that the carrying value of an asset may not be recoverable from the estimated future cash flows expected to result from its use and eventual disposition. We typically estimate the fair value of assets starting with a "Replacement Cost New" approach and then deduct appropriate amounts for both functional and economic obsolescence to arrive at the fair value estimates. Other factors considered by management in performing this assessment may include current operating results, trends, prospects, and third-party appraisals, as well as the effect of demand, competition, and other economic, legal, and regulatory factors. In estimating expected future cash flows for determining whether an asset is impaired, assets are grouped at the lowest level of identifiable cash flows, which, for most of our assets, is the individual property. These analyses are sensitive to management assumptions and the estimates of obsolescence factors. Changes in these assumptions and estimates could have a material impact on the analyses and the consolidated financial statements.

Additions to property and equipment are stated at cost. We capitalize the costs of improvements that extend the life of the asset. We expense maintenance and repair costs as incurred. Gains or losses on the dispositions of property and equipment are recognized in the period of disposal. Interest expense is capitalized on internally constructed assets at the applicable weighted average borrowing rates of interest. Capitalization of interest ceases when the project is substantially complete or construction activity is suspended for more than a brief period of time.

SAMPLE DISCLOSURE – REWARDS PROGRAM LIABILITY

The company's loyalty program offers incentives to customers who gamble at our casino entertainment facilities for on-property entertainment expenses, including gaming, hotel, dining, and retail shopping. Under the program, customers are able to accumulate, or bank, reward credits over time that they may redeem at their discretion under the terms of the program. The reward credit balance will be forfeited if the customer does not earn a reward credit over the prior six-month period. As a result of the ability of the customer to bank the reward credits, we accrue the estimated cost of fulfilling the redemption of reward credits, after consideration of estimated forfeitures (referred to as "breakage"), as they are earned. The estimated value of reward credits is expensed as the reward credits are earned by customers and is included in direct casino expense. To arrive at the estimated cost associated with reward credits, estimates and assumptions are made regarding incremental marginal costs of the benefits, breakage rates, and the mix of goods and services for which reward credits will be redeemed. We use historical data to assist in the determination of estimated accruals.

In addition to reward credits, customers can earn points based on play that are redeemable in the form of credits playable at the gaming machine. We accrue the cost of redeemable points, after consideration of estimated breakage, as they are earned. The cost is recorded as contra-revenue and is included in casino promotional allowances.

Profit Center Reporting

While the financial statements are quite useful, a casino manager can learn a great deal more about operations if the income statement is separated into a cluster of profit center income statements.

A profit center is a business unit within an organization that generates its own identifiable revenues, expenses, and profits or losses. Some of the more obvious profit centers within a full-service casino for which profit center reporting can be instituted are:

- Gaming tables
- Slot machines
- Keno
- Bingo
- Race and sports
- Bar
- Restaurants
- Hotel

In addition, it may be worthwhile to create a specialized profit center income statement for high-limit play. This is the part of a casino in which high rollers play, using very high wagers. This aspect of a casino's operations is quite different from its more traditional business segments, for high rollers demand expensive comps, and there is a risk that they will occasionally collect winnings that can trigger substantial losses for the casino. On the other hand, high roller losses can also be

171

substantial, accounting for a large part of the total profits of a casino. Consequently, management should see a profit center report for high rollers, if only to decide whether to continue catering to these types of players.

Internal reporting tends to be quite frequent. There may be a report of overall casino win by shift or gaming day, as well as by profit center within the casino for each shift. The reason for such frequent reporting is that management can use it to detect and follow up on issues immediately, before a problem results in the loss of an excessive amount of cash.

Other Accounting Reports

While the primary reporting function of the accounting department is the financial statements, there are a number of additional reports that can be produced for internal consumption. Here is a sampling of what can be produced to help the management team oversee casino operations, with the intent of focusing attention on activity levels, machine replacement decisions, and possible error situations:

- Comparison of actual to theoretical hold percentage by game, table, and dealer
- Comparison of slot meter readings to actual hard and soft count totals
- List of machines with highest win and loss deviations from the theoretical win percentage
- Popularity listing of machines in declining order by coin-in total
- Slot machine listing, including age, location, and machine type
- Summary of all activity for each individual slot machine, including slot drop and jackpot totals
- Summary of year-to-date and period-to-date win totals

Summary

The bulk of this chapter has been used to address the layout and content of the financial statements. From the perspective of the outside world, the financial statements are the primary work product of the accounting department. However, from an internal perspective, management is much more likely to be interested in profit center and related reports. These reports provide immediate feedback regarding potential problems within the casino and its support functions, which can be used to manage the business and yield more robust profits.

Chapter 11
Reporting Requirements

Introduction

A casino is subjected to special reporting requirements by the federal government, because it is considered a financial institution under the Bank Secrecy Act (BSA). These requirements were imposed because a casino deals with massive amounts of cash, and so is an obvious place for people to go when they want to launder cash. In this chapter, we cover the treatment of casinos as financial institutions, the Currency Transaction Report, and the Suspicious Activity Report. We also note the payroll reporting requirements that are particular to casinos – the Form W-2G and the 1099-MISC.

Treatment as a Financial Institution

The federal government has been deeply concerned with the laundering of cash by drug traffickers, and so passed the Bank Secrecy Act in 1970 to require financial institutions to prevent and detect money laundering.

Casinos deal with large amounts of cash every day, being involved in the following activities with their customers:
- Acceptance of funds for deposit and withdrawals of funds on deposit
- Check cashing services
- Currency exchanges
- Issuance of checks
- Issuance of credit and receipts of payments on credit
- Wire transfers of funds

Because of these activities, casinos are classified as financial institutions for the reporting purposes of the Bank Secrecy Act. This classification is detailed by the Internal Revenue Service as follows:

> Casinos and card clubs licensed to do business as casinos or card clubs and which have gross annual gaming revenues (GAGR) in excess of $1,000,000 are financial institutions subject to the requirements of the Bank Secrecy Act, which is known as Title 31.
>
> Casinos and card clubs on Indian lands with GAGR in excess of $1,000,000 are [also] defined as financial institutions...

Casinos sometimes maintain branch offices that serve as marketing offices; however, they may also accept funds from customers that are to be deposited in customer casino accounts or in payment of markers. Because of this additional financial activity, the Bank Secrecy Act applies to the branch offices of casinos.

That portion of the Code of Federal Regulations pertaining to the involvement of casinos in the reporting of money laundering situations is as follows:

§ 103.22 Reports of currency transactions.

Each casino shall file a report of each deposit, withdrawal, exchange of currency, gambling tokens or chips, or other payment or transfer, by, through or to such casino which involves a transaction in currency of more than $10,000. Multiple currency transactions shall be treated as a single transaction if the casino has knowledge that they are by or on behalf of any person and result in either cash in or cash out totaling more than $10,000 during any twenty-four hour period.

§ 103.36 Additional records to be made and retained by casinos.

Where a person is a nonresident alien, the casino shall also record the person's passport number or a description of some other government document used to verify his identity.

Currency Transaction Report

When a casino employee notes a situation in which a cash transaction exceeds $10,000 in a single business day, a Currency Transaction Report (CTR) must be filled out. The source of these reports can be a single transaction or a combination of cash transactions. The report is filed electronically with the Financial Crimes Enforcement Network (FinCEN). The reporting of information in the form is segregated into cash in and cash out transactions. Examples of "cash in" transactions include:

- Purchases of chips, tokens and other gaming instruments
- Front money deposits
- Safekeeping deposits
- Payments on any form of credit, including markers and counter checks
- Bets of currency
- Currency received for transmittal of funds through wire transfer for a customer
- Purchases of a casino's check
- Exchanges of currency for currency, including foreign currency

Examples of "cash out" transactions include:

- Redemptions of chips, tokens, and other gaming instruments
- Front money withdrawals
- Safekeeping withdrawals
- Advances on any form of credit, including markers and counter checks
- Payments on bets, including slot jackpots
- Payments by a casino to a customer based on receipt of funds through wire transfer for credit to a customer
- Cashing of checks or other negotiable instruments

174

- Exchanges of currency for currency, including foreign currency
- Reimbursements for customers' travel and entertainment expenses by the casino
- Payments for tournament, contest or other promotions

Additional points regarding the CTR are:
- The form must be filed when there is a transaction involving either cash received or cash disbursed of more than $10,000 in one day.
- Multiple transactions must be treated as one transaction when the casino has knowledge that the transactions are made by or on behalf of the same person.
- Reportable transactions may occur at a casino cage, gaming table, or slot machine.
- Do not file the form for cash-in when it is the same currency previously wagered in a money play on the same table game without leaving the table.
- Do not file the form for cash-out when it is won in a money play when it is the same currency wagered at the same table game without leaving the table.
- Anyone conducting a reportable transaction must be identified via an official or otherwise reliable record. Examples of official records are a driver's license, military identification card, passport, or alien registration card.
- Copies of all CTRs must be retained for at least five years.
- Cash-in and cash-out transactions for the same customer should be aggregated separately; they are not offset against each other.

EXAMPLE

Mr. Jones deposits $8,000 in currency to his front money account and pays $6,000 in currency to resolve an outstanding credit balance owed to the casino. He also receives $5,000 in currency from a wire transfer and cashes a check for $3,000, while also exchanging Euros for $2,500.

The $8,000 deposit and $6,000 payment are classified as cash-in, and aggregate to more than $10,000. These are reportable on a CTR.

The $5,000 wire transfer, $3,000 cashed check, and currency exchange of $2,500 are classified as cash-out, and aggregate to more than $10,000. These are reportable on a CTR.

A sample CTR form follows.

Form 103 – Currency Transaction Report by Casinos (page 1)

FINCEN Form **103**	**Currency Transaction Report by Casinos**	
(March 2011)	▶ Previous editions will not be accepted after September 2011.	
Department of the Treasury FINCEN	▶ Please type or print. Items marked with an asterisk* are considered critical. (See instructions.)	
	(Complete all applicable parts--See instructions)	OMB No. 1506-0005

1 If this is an amended report check here ☐ and complete the form in its entirety.

Part I   Person(s) Involved in Transaction(s)

Section A--Person(s) on Whose Behalf Transaction(s) Is Conducted (Customer)   2 ☐ Multiple persons

*3 Individual's last name or Organization's name	*4 First name	5 M.I.

6 Doing business as (DBA)

*7 Permanent address (number, street, and apt. or suite no.)	*8 SSN or EIN

*9 City	*10 State	*11 ZIP code	*12 Country code (if not U.S.)	*13 Date of birth MM DD YYYY

*14 Method used to verify identity: a ☐ Examined identification credential/document   b ☐ Known Customer - information on file   c ☐ Organization

*15 Describe identification credential: a ☐ Driver's license/State ID   b ☐ Passport   c ☐ Alien registration   z ☐ Other
Issued by: Number:

16 Customer's Account Number

Section B--Individual(s) Conducting Transaction(s) - If other than above (Agent)   17 ☐ Multiple agents

18 Individual's last name	19 First name	20 M.I.

21 Address (number, street, and apt. or suite no.)	22 SSN

23 City	24 State	25 ZIP code	26 Country code (if not U.S.)	27 Date of birth MM DD YYYY

28 Method used to verify identity: a ☐ Examined identification credential/document   b ☐ Known Customer - information on file

29 Describe identification credential: a ☐ Driver's license/State ID   b ☐ Passport   c ☐ Alien registration   z ☐ Other
Issued by: Number:

Part II   Amount and Type of Transaction(s). Complete all items that apply.   30 ☐ Multiple transactions

*31 CASH IN: (in U.S. dollar equivalent)		*32 CASH OUT: (in U.S. dollar equivalent)	
a Purchase(s) of casino chips, tokens, and other gaming instruments	$ .00	a Redemption(s) of casino chips, tokens, TITO tickets, and other gaming instruments	$ .00
b Deposit(s) (front money or safekeeping)	.00	b Withdrawal(s) of deposit (front money or safekeeping)	.00
c Payment(s) on credit (including markers)	.00	c Advance(s) on credit (including markers)	.00
d Currency wager(s) including money plays	.00	d Payment(s) on wager(s) (Including race book and OTB or sports pool)	.00
e Currency received from wire transfer(s) out	.00	e Currency paid from wire transfer(s) in	.00
f Purchase(s) of casino check(s)	.00	f Negotiable instrument(s) cashed (including checks)	.00
g Currency exchange(s)	.00	g Currency exchange(s)	.00
h Bills inserted into gaming devices	.00	h Travel and complimentary expenses and gaming incentives	.00
z Other (specify):	.00	i Payment for tournament, contest or other promotions	.00
		z Other (specify):	.00
Enter total of CASH IN transaction(s)	$ 0.00	Enter total of CASH OUT transaction(s)	$ 0.00

*33 Date of transaction (see instructions) MM DD YYYY	34 Foreign currency used: (Country)

Part III   Casino Reporting Transactions

*35 Casino's trade name	*36 Casino's legal name	*37 Employer Identification Number (EIN)

*38 Address where transaction occurred (See instructions)	*39 City

*40 State	*41 ZIP code	*42 Type of gaming Institution (Check only one) a ☐ State licensed casino b ☐ Card club c ☐ Tribal authorized casino z ☐ Other (specify)

Sign ▶ Here	43 Title of approving official	44 Signature of approving official	45 Date of signature MM DD YYYY
	46 Type or print preparer's name	47 Type or print name of person to contact	48 Contact telephone number ( )

Form 103 – Currency Transaction Report by Casinos (page 2)

Multiple Persons or Multiple Agents

(Complete applicable parts below if box 2 or box 17 on page 1 is checked.)

Part I	Person(s) Involved in Transaction(s)

Section A--Person(s) on Whose Behalf Transaction(s) Is Conducted (Customer)

*3 Individual's last name or Organization's name	*4 First name	5 M.I.

6 Doing business as (DBA)

*7 Permanent address (number, street, and apt. or suite no.)	*8 SSN or EIN

*9 City	*10 State	*11 ZIP code	*12 Country (if not U.S.)	*13 Date of birth MM DD YYYY

*14 Method used to verify identity: a ☐ Examined identification credential/document   b ☐ Known Customer - information on file   c ☐ Organization

*15 Describe identification credential: a ☐ Driver's license/State ID   b ☐ Passport   c ☐ Alien registration   z ☐ Other
Issued by: _____ Number: _____

16 Customer's Account Number

Section B--Individual(s) Conducting Transaction(s) - If other than above (Agent)

18 Individual's last name	19 First name	20 M.I.

21 Address (number, street, and apt. or suite no.)	22 SSN

23 City	24 State	25 ZIP code	26 Country (if not U.S.)	27 Date of birth MM DD YYYY

28 Method used to verify identity: a ☐ Examined identification credential/document   b ☐ Known Customer - information on file

29 Describe identification credential: a ☐ Driver's license/State ID   b ☐ Passport   c ☐ Alien registration   z ☐ Other
Issued by: _____ Number: _____

Suspicious Activity Report

A Suspicious Activity Report (SAR) is filed whenever a customer is suspected of trying to avoid the requirements of the Bank Secrecy Act, such as by engaging in money laundering. The report is filed with FinCEN. The FinCEN guidelines regarding when to file such a report are as follows:

> A casino [should] file a Casino SAR for any transaction conducted or attempted by, at, or through a casino, and involving or aggregating at least $5,000 in funds or other assets, that the casino knows, suspects, or has reason to suspect:
> - Involves funds derived from illegal activity or is intended or conducted in order to hide or disguise funds or assets derived from illegal activity (money laundering);
> - Is designed to evade the reporting or recordkeeping requirements of the BSA;
> - Has no business or apparent lawful purpose or is not the sort in which the particular customer would normally be expected to engage, and the casino knows of no reasonable explanation for the transaction after examining the available facts; or
> - Involves use of the casino to facilitate criminal activity.

A casino has 30 calendar days to file a SAR after the date of initial detection of any suspicious transaction or pattern of suspicious transactions or activities that are required to be reported. If the casino is unable to identify a suspect on the date it initially became aware of the suspicious transaction, the filer has an additional 30 calendar days to file, but in any circumstance, a SAR must be filed within 60 calendar days.

Here are several situations involving money laundering that might call for the filing of an SAR:

- *Minimal gaming.* An individual may possess stolen cash for which the bills are sequentially numbered, and therefore highly traceable. The person can swap these bills for other bills by converting them to chips at the cage, playing very little (to avoid gaming losses), and then cashing in the chips in exchange for different bills.
- *Initial marker with minimal gaming.* A variation on the preceding approach is to draw large casino markers to purchase chips, then playing very little, and then paying off the markers in currency. The remaining chips are then redeemed for a casino check.
- *Minimal slot machine usage.* A person could insert currency into a slot machine currency validator, engage in a minimal amount of gaming activity, and then cash out for a casino check, thereby converting currency to a check.

Additional points regarding the SAR are:

- Casinos must use it to report suspicious activities involving or aggregating at least $5,000.
- When a reportable transaction is ongoing, the casino has an obligation to immediately notify the applicable law enforcement and regulatory authorities by telephone.
- The casino cannot notify any person involved in a transaction that he or she has been reported.
- If a currency transaction is greater than $10,000 and is suspicious, the casino must file both a CTR and a SAR. If the transaction is for $10,000 or less, then only a SAR must be filed.
- Supporting documentation is not to be filed with a SAR. Instead, retain it along with a copy of the relevant SAR for at least five years. Examples of supporting documentation are:

Canceled checks	Deposit slips	Identification credentials
Confessions	Multiple transaction logs	Photographs
Credit bureau reports	Player rating records	Surveillance videos
Credit slips	Slot club records	Withdrawal slips

A sample SAR form follows.

Form 102 – Suspicious Activity Report (page 1)

FinCEN **Form 102** March 2011 Previous editions will not be accepted after September 30, 2011	**Suspicious Activity Report** **by Casinos and Card Clubs** ▶ Please type or print. Always complete entire report. Items marked with an asterisk * are considered critical (see instructions).	OMB No. 1506 - 0006

1 Check the box if this report corrects a prior report (see instructions on page 6) ☐

Part I	**Subject Information**	2 Check box (a) ☐ if more than one subject	box (b) ☐ subject information unavailable

*3 Individual's last name or entity's full name	*4 First name	5 Middle initial

6 also known as (AKA- individual), doing business as (DBA- entity)	7 Occupation / type of business

*8 Address	*9 City

*10 State	*11 ZIP code	*12 Country (if not U.S.)	13 Vehicle license # / state (optional) a. number b. state

*14 SSN / ITIN (individual) or EIN (entity)	*15 Account number No account affected ☐ Account open ? Yes ☐ No ☐	16 Date of birth MM DD YYYY

*17 Government issued identification (if available) a ☐ Driver's license/state ID b ☐ Passport d ☐ Alien registration
d ☐ Other _____
e Number: |__|__|__|__|__|__|__|__|__|__|__|__|__| f Issuing state or country_____

18 Phone number - work ( ) -	19 Phone number - home ( ) -	20 E-mail address (if available)

21 Affiliation or relationship to casino/card club
a ☐ Customer b ☐ Agent c ☐ Junket / tour operator d ☐ Employee e ☐ Check cashing operator
f ☐ Supplier g ☐ Concessionaire h ☐ Other (Explain in Part VI)

22 Does casino/card club still have a business association and/or an employee/employer relationship with suspect? a ☐ Yes b ☐ No If **no**, why? c ☐ Barred d ☐ Resigned e ☐ Terminated f ☐ Other (Specify in Part VI)	23 Date action taken(22) / / MM DD YYYY

Part II	**Suspicious Activity Information**

*24 Date or date range of suspicious activity From ___/___/___ To ___/___/___ MM DD YYYY MM DD YYYY	*25 Total dollar amount involved in suspicious activity $|__|__|__|__|__|__|__|__|__|.00

* 26 Type of suspicious activity:
a ☐ Bribery/gratuity
b ☐ Check fraud (includes counterfeit)
c ☐ Credit/debit card fraud (incl. counterfeit)
d ☐ Embezzlement/theft
e ☐ Large currency exchange(s)
f ☐ Minimal gaming with large transactions
g ☐ Misuse of position
h ☐ Money laundering
i ☐ No apparent business or lawful purpose
j ☐ Structuring
k ☐ Unusual use of negotiable instruments (checks)
l ☐ Use of multiple credit or deposit accounts
m ☐ Unusual use of wire transfers
n ☐ Unusual use of counter checks or markers
o ☐ False or conflicting ID(s)
p ☐ Terrorist financing
q ☐ Other (Describe in Part VI)

Part III	**Law Enforcement or Regulatory Contact Information**

27 If law enforcement or a regulatory agency has been contacted (excluding submission of a SARC), check the appropriate box.
a ☐ DEA
b ☐ U.S. Attorney (** 28)
c ☐ IRS
d ☐ FBI
e ☐ U.S. Customs Service
f ☐ U.S. Secret Service
g ☐ Local law enforcement
h ☐ State gaming commission
i ☐ State law enforcement
j ☐ Tribal gaming commission
k ☐ Tribal law enforcement
l ☐ Other (List in item 28)

28 Other authority contacted (for box 27 g through l) ** List U.S. Attorney office here.	29 Name of person contacted (for all of box 27)

30 Telephone number of individual contacted in box 29 ( ) -	31 Date Contacted / / MM DD YYYY

Form 102 – Suspicious Activity Report (page 2)

Part IV	Reporting Casino or Card Club Information		2

*32 Trade name of casino or card club	*33 Legal name of casino or card club	*34 EIN

*35 Address

*36 City	*37 State	*38 ZIP code

39 Type of gaming institution

a ☐ State licensed casino   b ☐ Tribal licensed casino   c ☐ Card club   d ☐ Other (s pecify)_____

Part V	Contact for Assistance

*40 Last name of individual to be contacted regarding this report	*41 First name	42 Middle initial

*43 Title/Position	*44 Work phone number	*45 Date report prepared
	( ) -	___/___/___ MM DD YYYY

Part VI	Suspicious Activity Information - Narrative*

Explanation/description of suspicious activity(ies). This section of the report is critical. The care with which it is completed may determine whether or not the described activity and its possible criminal nature are clearly understood by investigators. Provide a clear, complete and chronological description (**not exceeding this page and the next page**) of the activity, including what is unusual, irregular, or suspicious about the transaction(s), using the checklist below as a guide as you prepare your account.

a. **Describe** the conduct that raised suspicion.

b. **Explain** whether the transaction(s) was completed or only attempted.

c. **Describe** supporting documentation and retain such documentation for your file for five years.

d. **Explain** who benefited, financially or otherwise, from the transaction(s), how much and how (if known).

e. **Describe and retain** any admission or explanation of the transaction(s) provided by the subject(s), witness(s), or other person(s). Indicate to whom and when it was given. Include witness or other person ID.

f. **Describe and retain** any evidence of cover-up or evidence of an attempt to deceive federal or state examiners, or others.

g. **Indicate** where the possible violation of law(s) took place (e.g., branch, cage, specific gaming pit, specific gaming area).

h. **Indicate** whether the suspicious activity is an isolated incident or relates to another transaction.

i. **Indicate** whether there is any related litigation. If so, specify the name of the litigation and the court where the action is pending.

j. **Recommend** any further investigation that might assist law enforcement authorities.

k. **Indicate** whether any information has been excluded from this report; if so, state reasons.

l. **Indicate** whether any U.S. or foreign currency and/or U.S. or foreign negotiable instrument(s) were involved. If foreign, provide the amount, name of currency, and country of origin.

m. **Indicate** whether funds or assets were recovered and, if so, enter the dollar value of the recovery in whole dollars only.

n. **Indicate** any additional account number(s), and any domestic or foreign bank(s) account numbers which may be involved.

o. **Indicate** for a foreign national any available information on subject's passport(s), visa(s), and/or identification card(s). Include date, country, city of issue, issuing authority, and nationality.

p. **Describe** any suspicious activities that involve transfer of funds to or from a foreign country, or any exchanges of a foreign currency. Identify the currency, country, sources and destinations of funds.

q. **Describe** subject(s) position if employed by the casino or card club (e.g., dealer, pit supervisor, cage cashier, host, etc.).

r. **Indicate** the type of casino or card club filing this report, if this is not clear from Part IV.

s. **Describe** the subject only if you do not have the identifying information in Part 1 or if multiple individuals use the same identification. Use descriptors such as male, female, age, etc.

t. **Indicate** any wire transfer in or out identifier numbers, including the transfer company's name.

u. **If correcting** a prior report, complete the form in its entirety and note the changes here in Part VI.

NOTE: Information already provided in earlier parts of this form need not necessarily be repeated if the meaning is clear.

Tips on SAR Form preparation and filing are available in the SAR Activity Review at www.fincen.gov/pub_reports.html.

Supporting documentation should not be filed with this report. Maintain the information for your files.

Do not include legal disclaimers in this narrative. Continue on next page as necessary.

FinCEN provides multiple examples of how the narrative section of the SAR should be filled out, with an emphasis on providing a sufficient level of detail to justify the report and to assist with subsequent legal activities. One of the examples used by FinCEN in its *Suspicious Activity Reporting Guidance for Casinos* brochure is:

Customer A, Casino account # xxxxx, approached the casino cage at approximately 11:40 PM on 0/0/00 asking about reportable transactions. The cashier noticed that he had two brown chips ($5,000 denomination) in his hand but didn't cash them. He returned to cash in $2,800 in small denomination chips.

At 5:15 AM, a man named B came to the cage to cash in $10,000 in brown chips but there was no verification of him having played. It was decided to cash him out. The pit personnel saw him walk to Customer A and hand the cash to A.

At 5:30 AM a woman named C came to the cage to cash in one brown $5,000 chip. Again, no verification of play was found and the customer acted uneasy. The pit allowed the cash out and again noticed C walk directly to A and hand him the cash.

It is the belief of the pit and the cage, as a result, that Customer A was structuring the transaction and using paid agents to circumvent reporting requirements.[1]

Customer Reporting Avoidance Strategies

The strategies most commonly employed by individuals attempting to circumvent the $10,000 reporting rules are as follows:

- *Structuring.* A person breaks up a large monetary transaction into a number of smaller ones. Thus, a person could deposit $2,000 at the cage six times during a day, which is called structuring. This approach can be spotted by maintaining a multiple transaction log (see the next section) and searching it for multiple entries.
- *Gaming day overlap.* The $10,000 reporting threshold for the CTR is based on the gaming day employed by a casino, which can be any 24-hour period. If a customer knows the exact timing of the gaming day, he could engage in cash in or cash out transactions that span two days, and so drop below the daily $10,000 reporting threshold. For example, if the gaming day ends at 10 p.m., a person could exchange $6,000 of foreign currency just before 10 p.m., and then do so again just after 10 p.m., and these cash out transactions would not be reportable, since they do not sum to $10,000 on the same gaming day. However, they are reportable on a SAR.

> **Note:** In order to avoid the amount of CTR reporting, some casinos figure out the average period of play for their customers, and select a game day that ends in the middle of this period. Doing so splits the period of play into different reporting periods.

- *Agent involvement.* An individual could have several associates handle cash-in or out transactions on his behalf, which in aggregate total to more than the

---

[1] Reproduced with permission.

$10,000 threshold. It may require detailed surveillance to discern the existence of agents.

- *Multiple accounts.* A customer maintains more than one account at a casino, and keeps cash transactions below $10,000 for each of these accounts. An alias may be used for the additional accounts.
- *Fake ID.* A customer could provide a fake identification document to a casino, so that any CTR is not connected with the customer.
- *Multiple tables.* A player could move among multiple tables, always limiting the buy-in at each table to less than $10,000. This approach is less effective when records are stored and updated centrally.

In addition, someone could use a casino in order to engage in structuring with other financial institutions. For example, a person could withdraw a large amount of funds from a deposit account and request that the money be paid out in the form of a large number of smaller casino checks, all below the threshold for CTR reporting.

Transaction Tracking

There are a number of recordation systems within a casino that can be used to locate transactions that may be reportable on a CTR. They are noted within the following sub-sections.

Multiple Transaction Log

The multiple transaction log (MTL) is used to keep track of cash transactions above a certain minimum threshold. The intent of recording these transactions in the log is to identify any cash in or out events that should be aggregated, and which would then be reported on a CTR as being more than $10,000.

An MTL should be maintained in all areas of a casino that handle cash in and cash out transactions. At the end of the gaming day, all MTLs are forwarded to the accounting department, where they are examined to see if any CTRs must be generated. Alternatively, these reports can be examined on-site during the gaming day to see if any CTR events have occurred. A new MTL is then used for the next gaming day.

The information on an MTL should include the following:
- Report header
  - Report date
  - Report location
- Transaction information
  - Customer name
  - Customer description
  - Transaction time
  - Transaction amount
  - Transaction type
  - Table number (if applicable)
  - Clerk signature

An MTL may be incorporated into the computer systems of a casino, in which case the system will automatically create notifications of CTR events.

Check Register

A check register is maintained for all casino checks issued to customers, sometimes with a short description of the reason for each check payment. This information can be used to compile cash-out transactions for a CTR.

Credit Management System

A credit management system (CMS) is used to monitor the account-related activities of those customers who maintain deposit or credit accounts with a casino. The transactions populating a CMS originate with cage cashiers, and typically include:
- Deposit slips, noting funds deposited into a customer's account
- Withdrawal slips, noting each individual withdrawal from a customer's account
- Markers issued, noting the extension of credit to a customer
- Other payment/redemption vouchers, noting such transactions as marker redemptions (paydowns of outstanding credit), reimbursements of customer travel expenses, and foreign currency exchanges

The information in a CMS can be used as the basis for a CTR, since CMS transactions usually split out that portion of each transaction that involves currency.

Player Rating System

A player rating system (PRS) is a database used by a casino to track the gaming activity of its customers. A floor person prepares a player rating card for each rated customer at a table, which is later added to the PRS database. The rating card identifies a customer, pit and table location, and the amount of currency received from the customer in the form of cash bets and for the purchase of chips. The estimated average bet and hours played are also noted.

The intent of a PRS is to make a determination from gaming activity regarding the level of complimentary services that will be offered to certain customers in order to entice them to play further, as well as to send them marketing materials. Though the PRS is intended to be a marketing tool for rewarding the best customers, it can also be used as an information source for calculating cash-in from a customer, which can then be used for a CTR.

Wire Transfer Log

A casino may receive funds via wire transfer on behalf of its customers, as well as issue wire transfers as per customer instructions. These transactions, including wiring instructions, are recorded in a wire transfer log. The information in this log can be used to determine cash in and cash out amounts for customers, which may be used for a CTR.

Winnings Reporting Forms

A casino must furnish a Form W-2G to a player if the player receives any of the following:
- $1,200 or more in gambling winnings from bingo or slot machines;
- $1,500 or more in proceeds from keno (this is the amount of winnings minus the amount of the wager);
- More than $5,000 in winnings from a poker tournament (reduced by the wager or buy-in);
- $600 or more in gambling winnings (excluding the preceding items) where the payout is at least 300 times the amount of the wager; or
- Any other gambling winnings subject to federal income tax withholding.

This form is completed on-the-spot when winnings occur, not following the end of the calendar year. A sample Form W-2G follows.

Sample Form W-2G – Certain Gambling Winnings

PAYER'S name, street address, city or town, province or state, country, and ZIP or foreign postal code		1 Gross winnings $	2 Date won	OMB No. 1545-0238 2016
		3 Type of wager $	4 Federal income tax withheld $	Form W-2G
		5 Transaction	6 Race	Certain Gambling Winnings
		7 Winnings from identical wagers $	8 Cashier	
PAYER'S federal identification number	PAYER'S telephone number	9 Winner's taxpayer identification no.	10 Window	
WINNER'S name		11 First I.D.	12 Second I.D.	For Privacy Act and Paperwork Reduction Act Notice, see the 2016 General Instructions for Certain Information Returns.
Street address (including apt. no.)		13 State/Payer's state identification no.	14 State winnings $	
City or town, province or state, country, and ZIP or foreign postal code		15 State income tax withheld $	16 Local winnings $	File with Form 1096
		17 Local income tax withheld $	18 Name of locality	Copy A For Internal Revenue Service Center

Under penalties of perjury, I declare that, to the best of my knowledge and belief, the name, address, and taxpayer identification number that I have furnished correctly identify me as the recipient of this payment and any payments from identical wagers, and that no other person is entitled to any part of these payments.

Signature ▶   Date ▶

Form **W-2G**   Cat. No. 10138V   www.irs.gov/w2g   Department of the Treasury - Internal Revenue Service

It may be necessary for a casino to also withhold a portion of an award and forward it to the IRS, if a customer cannot provide proper identification. Withholding is more likely if an individual is not a resident of the United States. If so, the withholding is reported on Form 1042S. A sample Form 1042S follows, with the amount withheld noted in Box 7a (which is highlighted).

Sample Form 1042-S – Foreign Person's U.S. Source Income Subject to Withholding

Form **1042-S**	Foreign Person's U.S. Source Income Subject to Withholding			20**16**	OMB No. 1545-0096
Department of the Treasury Internal Revenue Service	▶ Information about Form 1042-S and its separate instructions is at www.irs.gov/form1042s.				**Copy A** for Internal Revenue Service
	☐ ☐ ☐ AMENDED		☐ ☐ ☐ PRO-RATA BASIS REPORTING		

1 Income code	2 Gross income	3 Chapter indicator. Enter "3" or "4"		13e Recipient's U.S. TIN, if any			
		3a Exemption code	4a Exemption code	13f Ch. 3 status code		13g Ch. 4 status code	
		3b Tax rate .	4b Tax rate .	13h Recipient's GIIN	13i Recipient's foreign tax identification number, if any		13j LOB code
5 Withholding allowance							
6 Net income		7b Check if tax not deposited with IRS pursuant to escrow procedure ☐		13k Recipient's account number			13l Recipient's date of birth
7a Federal tax withheld							
8 Tax withheld by other agents				14a Primary Withholding Agent's Name (if applicable)			
9 Tax paid by withholding agent							
10 Total withholding credit				14b Primary Withholding Agent's EIN			
11 Amount repaid to recipient				15a Intermediary or flow-through entity's EIN, if any		15b Ch. 3 status code	15c Ch. 4 status code
12a Withholding agent's EIN		12b Ch. 3 status code	12c Ch. 4 status code				
12d Withholding agent's name				15d Intermediary or flow-through entity's name			
12e Withholding agent's Global Intermediary Identification Number (GIIN)				15e Intermediary or flow-through entity's GIIN			
12f Country code		12g Foreign taxpayer identification number, if any		15f Country code	15g Foreign tax identification number, if any		
12h Address (number and street)				15h Address (number and street)			
12i City or town, state or province, country, ZIP or foreign postal code				15i City or town, state or province, country, ZIP or foreign postal code			
13a Recipient's name		13b Recipient's country code		16a Payer's name		16b Payer's TIN	
13c Address (number and street)				16c Payer's GIIN		16d Ch. 3 status code	16e Ch. 4 status code
13d City or town, state or province, country, ZIP or foreign postal code				17a State income tax withheld	17b Payer's state tax no.	17c Name of state	

The amount to be withheld from the award to a non-qualifying person is 30%, unless the recipient is from a treaty country. The gambling income of a treaty country is not taxable by the United States[2]. These countries are:

List of Treaty Countries Whose Residents' Gambling Income is not Taxable

Austria	Iceland	Slovak Republic
Belgium	Ireland	Slovenia
Bulgaria	Italy	South Africa
Czech Republic	Japan	Spain
Denmark	Latvia	Sweden
Finland	Lithuania	Tunisia
France	Luxembourg	Turkey
Germany	Netherlands	Ukraine
Hungary	Russia	United Kingdom

Proceeds from a wager placed in blackjack, baccarat, craps, roulette, or big-6 wheel are not amounts subject to reporting.

---

[2] As noted in IRS Publication 515

A casino must furnish a Form 1099-MISC to a player if the player receives a prize or award that is not for services performed, or a payout from a tournament in which there was no entry fee. The amount of this payment is recorded in Box 3 (Other Income) of the form, for which a sample form follows, with Box 3 highlighted.

Sample Form 1099-MISC – Miscellaneous Income

PAYER'S name, street address, city or town, state or province, country, ZIP or foreign postal code, and telephone no.		1 Rents $	OMB No. 1545-0115	Miscellaneous Income
		2 Royalties $	2016	
			Form 1099-MISC	
		3 Other income $	4 Federal income tax withheld $	Copy A For
PAYER'S federal identification number	RECIPIENT'S identification number	5 Fishing boat proceeds	6 Medical and health care payments	Internal Revenue Service Center
		$	$	File with Form 1096.
RECIPIENT'S name		7 Nonemployee compensation	8 Substitute payments in lieu of dividends or interest	For Privacy Act and Paperwork Reduction Act
Street address (including apt. no.)		$	$	Notice, see the 2016 General
City or town, state or province, country, and ZIP or foreign postal code		9 Payer made direct sales of $5,000 or more of consumer products to a buyer (recipient) for resale ▶ ☐	10 Crop insurance proceeds $	Instructions for Certain Information Returns.
		11	12	
Account number (see instructions)	FATCA filing requirement ☐	2nd TIN not. ☐	13 Excess golden parachute payments $	14 Gross proceeds paid to an attorney $
15a Section 409A deferrals $	15b Section 409A income $	16 State tax withheld $	17 State/Payer's state no.	18 State income $

There may be instances in which a group of customers decides to split a jackpot. If so, the taxable earnings must be divided amongst the group, using IRS Form 5754. A sample of the top portion of the form follows. In essence, it identifies the person to whom winnings were paid, as well as the amount paid, and how that amount is apportioned among the group.

Sample Form 5754 – Statement by Person(s) Receiving Gambling Winnings

Form **5754** (Rev. December 2008) Department of the Treasury Internal Revenue Service	**Statement by Person(s) Receiving Gambling Winnings** ► Recipients of gambling winnings should see the instructions on the back of this form. ► Payers of gambling winnings should see the separate Instructions for Forms W-2G and 5754.	OMB No. 1545-0239 Return to payer. Do not send to the IRS.

Date won	Type of winnings	Game number	Machine number	Race number

Part I Person to Whom Winnings Are Paid

Name		Address	
Taxpayer identification number	Other I.D.	Amount received	Federal income tax withheld

Part II Persons to Whom Winnings Are Taxable *(continued on page 2)*

(a) Name	(b) Taxpayer identification number	(c) Address	(d) Amount won	(e) Winnings from identical wagers

Summary

The volume of cash that a casino routinely handles makes it virtually certain that a large number of Currency Transaction Reports will be filed on a regular basis. In addition, the Form W-2G will likely be issued many times, since the threshold for reporting winnings is so low. Consequently, a casino should have excellent procedures in place for how these forms are to be completed, when they will be issued, and who is responsible for the issuances. In addition, there should be a process in place for addressing any errors found on these reports, so that the errors do not recur in the future.

Glossary

A

Account. A separate, detailed record about a specific item.

Accounting equation. The concept that the total of all assets equals the total of all liabilities and shareholders' equity.

Allowance for doubtful accounts. A reserve that reduces the total amount of accounts receivable appearing on the balance sheet.

B

Balance sheet. A report that summarizes all of an entity's assets, liabilities, and equity as of a given point in time.

Bank. The inventory of bills, coins, and chips held by a casino.

Banked game. A game of chance in which the casino and its customers can both win or lose.

Base jackpot. The minimum fixed amount of a payout by a slot machine for a certain combination.

Betting ticket. A form used to record a wager, the date, and the related event.

Buy-in. The amount of funds used by a player to buy casino chips when beginning to play. A buy-in can be made with cash, credit, or a deposit withdrawal.

C

Cage. A secure work area in which a casino's bankroll is stored and cashiers work.

Cash conversion cycle. The time period required to convert resources into cash.

Cash equivalents. As used in a casino, the term refers to chips, which are non-financial instruments that are readily convertible into cash.

Chart of accounts. A listing of all the accounts used by an organization to record its business transactions.

Chip. A substitute for money that is issued by a gaming entity, and used in its wagering operations. A chip is a round, plastic disk that is color-coded to denote a certain value.

Chip redemption. The exchange of chips held by a customer for cash, a casino check, or an outbound wire transfer.

Coin-in. The amount of coins put into a slot machine by customers.

Comps. Complimentary goods and services issued to players to encourage them to gamble.

Credit memo. A document issued by the seller of goods or services, reducing the amount that a buyer owes to the seller under the terms of an earlier invoice.

Credit slip. A form used to document the return of excess chips to the cage from a gaming table.

Cross-fill. The transfer of chips from one gaming table to another.

D

Dealer. A casino employee who conducts a game.

Debt. An amount owed for funds borrowed.

Depreciation. The gradual charging to expense of an asset's cost over its useful life.

Direct write-off method. The practice of charging bad debts to expense in the period when individual markers have been identified as bad debts.

Double entry accounting. A record keeping system in which every transaction is recorded in at least two accounts.

Drop. The amount of revenue collected on all gambling activities, usually for a specific location within a casino, such as a gaming table.

Drop box. A locked container associated with a gaming table in which drop is stored.

Drop bucket. A container within a slot machine that collects excess coins and tokens.

Drop team. The cage employees who replace drop boxes on the casino floor.

E

Equity. The net amount of funds invested in a business by its owners, plus any retained earnings.

F

Fill. A transaction that transfers chips from the cage to a gaming table or slot machine.

Financial statements. A collection of reports that describe the financial results, condition, and cash flows of an entity.

Fixed asset. Assets providing an economic benefit over a long period of time.

Foreign chips. Chips issued by other casinos.

Free play. Free wagering that increases the odds that a customer may win.

Front money. Funds deposited by a customer into a personal account at a casino that can be withdrawn either at a gaming table or the cage.

G

Gaming day. The standard business day of a casino, for which it maintains its accounting records.

General ledger. The master set of all accounts, in which are stored all of the business transactions that have been entered into the accounts.

Gross gaming revenue. The difference between gaming wins and losses.

Gross pay. The amount of compensation to be paid to an employee before any deductions are withheld from the pay.

H

Hard count. The process of counting coins and tokens.

High roller. A gambler who wagers large amounts of money.

Hold. The amount of money that a casino retains after betting ceases. The formula for hold is drop minus paid outs. Hold matches the amount of money on hand.

Hold percentage. The proportion of gross gaming revenue to table drop.

Hopper. The tray within a slot machine that hold the coins used to pay out jackpots.

Host. A casino employee who handles relations with the more significant customers, with responsibility for issuing comps and assisting with the granting of credit.

I

Income statement. A financial report that summarizes an entity's revenue, cost of goods sold, gross margin, other costs, and net income or loss.

Interest capitalization. The inclusion of the interest cost of the debt associated with a project in the capital cost of that project.

J

Jackpot. Money won in a game of chance.

Jackpot payout. That part of a jackpot paid by a slot employee to a player; this amount is the difference between the amount directly paid by the slot machine and the total amount due.

Journal entry. A formalized method for recording a business transaction, used in a double entry accounting system.

K

Keno. A game of chance that is similar to lotto, and which uses a ball machine or a random number generator.

L

Ledger. A book or database in which double entry accounting transactions are stored or summarized.

M

Marker. A signed document that obligates a customer to repay a loan; the marker is then traded for gaming chips.

Marker redemption. The act of paying off a marker previously issued to a customer.

N

Net gaming revenue. Gross gaming revenues minus such cash sales incentives as discounts, match play, free play, and slot club points.

P

Paid outs. The money paid to a customer on a winning bet.

Pit. An area on the casino floor where gaming tables are situated.

Posting. The aggregation of financial transactions from where they are stored in subsidiary ledgers, and the transfer of this information into the general ledger.

Progressive jackpot. A jackpot for a gaming machine that increases each time a game is played, unless the customer wins the jackpot.

R

Racino. A race track that also offers gambling activities to its customers.

Rake-off. A fixed commission fee charged to poker players by a casino.

Rated player. A customer whose gaming activities are tracked through a casino's player rating system.

S

Short pay. When the hopper of a slot machine is emptied before the full amount of the jackpot has been paid.

Slot drop. The amount of currency retained by a slot machine, not including the amount retained in the hopper for payouts.

Slot machine. The mechanical device for gambling that is initiated by the insertion of money, and which pays off based on the matching of symbols on wheels that are spun by the machine.

Soft count. The process of counting bills.

Statement of cash flows. A part of the financial statements that summarizes an entity's cash inflows and outflows in relation to financing, operating, and investing activities.

T

TITO ticket. A ticket printed by a slot machine that can be redeemed for cash or used to fund additional play on other machines.

Token. A substitute for currency, used to play slot machines.

Trial balance. A report containing the ending balances of all accounts in the general ledger.

U

Useful life. The time period over which it is expected that an asset will be productive.

W

Wagering account. An electronic ledger for a customer, noting the person's deposits, withdrawals, and transfers to and from a game.

Win. The difference between gaming wins and losses, prior to the deduction of expenses.

Index

194

CPSIA information can be obtained
at www.ICGtesting.com
Printed in the USA
LVOW02s2109250716

497713LV00021B/388/P

9 781938 910678